the little book of
SHEFFIELD

A CELEBRATION OF THE AMAZING INDEPENDENTS ON YOUR DOORSTEP

CONTENTS

04 FOREWORD FROM HENDERSON'S RELISH

06 MAKE YOURSELF AT HOME

08 RESTAURANTS

50 PUBS + BARS

72 CAFÉS

100 MAKERS

146 RETAILERS

170 VENUES

FOREWORD
HENDERSON'S RELISH

Over the last decade or so, Sheffield's independent businesses have flourished, thanks to the enterprise and effort of some of our city's most creative commercial talents. Independent businesses benefit us all, boosting the local economy, providing valuable products and services, contributing to our community life and employing local workers. This book highlights some of Sheffield's brightest local businesses, celebrating the unique contributions they make to our city.

Henderson's Relish is perhaps Sheffield's best-known independent business. We have been part of the culinary and cultural life of the city for more than 100 years, and we are still mixing and bottling Sheffield's famous sauce to our secret recipe. Henderson's has survived and thrived because of its independence. Henderson's is 'Made in Sheffield', and it's made for Sheffield.

Henry Henderson created his 'Strong & Northern' sauce in 1885, when steel was at the heart of the city's culture. Networks of craftspeople called Little Mesters were forging, grinding and finishing in workshops not unlike our first factory, adding their unique contributions to some of the world's finest quality products.

This flair for creativity and industry lives on all around our city, in the family businesses, shops, cafés, pubs and bakeries that line our streets. Known as 'England's biggest village', Sheffield has always been independent in spirit. Sheffield's values are unique; we are fiercely proud yet generous in recognising and celebrating the treasures that make up our diverse and inclusive communities.

Our independent businesses serve us all, and today we need them more than ever. This year the coronavirus pandemic has turned all our lives upside down. It has shaken us, and continues to threaten much that we hold dear. Yet Sheffield has responded in the only way it knows: pulling together through this crisis just as we have before. Our independents show us what we can achieve when we each play our part, serving our neighbours and looking out for each other. It is in adversity that our community spirit shines brightest.

Matt Davies, Henderson's Relish

This flair for creativity and industry lives on all around our city, in the shops, cafés, breweries, bars, restaurants, hotels and bakeries that line our streets.

HOME,
SWEET HOME!

The Little Book of Sheffield is proudly supporting the Make Yourself at Home campaign launched by Sheffield City Council in 2020.

Make Yourself at Home is all about promoting pride in our city and sharing stories about the wonderful independent businesses, communities and institutions that make it such a special place to live.

The distinction between this and 'Open For Business' campaigns seen elsewhere is the acknowledgement that moving forward will be especially difficult for some groups and individuals in our communities. Therefore, it focuses on bringing them into the conversation, listening, providing reassurance, and truly uniting the city.

Councillor Julie Dore, Leader of Sheffield City Council, said of the campaign: "We want to create something that the people of the city, whether independent business owners, community centre leaders, cultural creators, entrepreneurs or individual residents, can understand, get behind and use to create a pride of place for Sheffield."

A homepage has been set up at *welcometosheffield.co.uk/makeyourselfathome* where businesses and organisations can download the Make Yourself at Home toolkit, which includes badges to use on artwork, images to share on social media and a guide to how the campaign can be used to suit a wide range of purposes.

Also available on the website is a wide range of content promoting the very best of what the Steel City has to offer during these difficult times. You can follow @VisitSheffield on Twitter, Facebook and Instagram for the latest updates on the campaign.

Have your say online by posting how #SheffieldMakes you feel at home.

RESTAURANTS

ASHOKA

Known across the city for its 'reyt good curreh' with a perfect fusion of Sheffield and India, Ashoka is a restaurant and takeaway that has always played by its own rules.

Established in 1967 on Ecclesall Road, the quirky independent recently earned a spot on The Times' list of best curry houses in Britain. It was also named in the 2018 edition of the Good Food Guide, one of only 52 Indian restaurants to be included. These accolades are testament to the quality of food as well as the unique personality that has endeared Sheffielders to the restaurant over the decades.

Kamal Ahmed, a young Bengali who had no industry experience except waiting tables, founded the curry house and introduced the real flavours of Indian cooking to the neighbourhood. Long before multiculturalism entered the mainstream, he was able to win diners over with radically different food. "It was seen as exotic," says the current owner, Rahul Amin. "He really went above and beyond in terms of the design of the place. Ashoka used to use silver cutlery made in Sheffield, which no one else did, and the menus were written by hand in calligraphy."

That flair for standing out in the crowd remains with Ashoka today. The restaurant recently got a new look inspired by the Irani cafés of Mumbai which features a monochrome tiled floor, tiffin boxes and wooden tables. These classic touches make it feel homely, unlike most other curry houses, and the menu reflects this too. You won't find the much-loved Taxi Driver Curry anywhere but Ashoka, because it was created specially by the restaurant. Karai, kashmiri and biryani jostle for diners' attention alongside lamb chops, chicken tikka and butter naans from the traditional charcoal tandoor.

The restaurant's tagline is 'inspired by India, made in Sheffield' and that really sums up the approach to its food, with menus comprising a mixture of British classics and traditional dishes from northern India.

AVAILABLE ON CITY GRAB
Ashoka
307 Ecclesall Road,
Sheffield, S11 8NX
0114 268 3029
ashoka1967.com

CUBANA

For the past 20 years Cubana has been a hot staple in Sheffield, with its Latin music, salsa dancing, tasty tapas food and Havana-filled cocktails, infusing a vibrant explosion of joy into a rainy English day.

Bringing colour to the city, Cubana is perfect for drinking and dining in a fun-filled environment. Inside you'll find a spacious bar filled with a variety of food, drink and music from around the world in its own cultural hub of its type in Sheffield.

Co-owner Adrian Bagnoli first discovered his passion for Latin music whilst visiting a Brazilian nightclub called the Maracanã in Florence, Italy. Falling in love with the lively atmosphere, he came to realise that this was what Sheffield needed. He started by launching Sheffield's first Latin club night "Viva Salsa" in 1995 at city centre night spot Club Uropa. In 2000 Adrian joined forces with Brad Charlesworth to open Cubana Tapas bar on Trippet Lane, where they were met with huge success before unleashing Cubana onto Leopold Square in 2014.

The eccentric atmosphere manifests into the culinary experience. Their extensive menu has won national acclaim, combining classic Spanish tapas with South American flair and flavour, which includes both meat and plant-based options. Cubana takes pride in its team of chefs, all with a wealth of experience, which explains why they are held in such high regard for top quality and consistency. Accompanying the tasty tapas comes an award-winning rum collection, quality wine list and a plethora of exotic cocktails, promising to add a liveliness and sparkle to your evening out.

When you think of Cubana you immediately think of live music; there's regular performances from local and nationally renowned musicians almost every night. They also regularly host dance classes from Cuban salsa to Argentinian tango, and Bachata from the Dominican Republic. With this in mind, Cubana organises one of the biggest outdoor salsa events in the country: 'Salsa In The Square', which takes place over three Bank Holiday Sundays each year and attracts hundreds of people for a mix of live Latin music, salsa displays, dancing and more. The event has become a cornerstone of Sheffield's cultural calendar.

During the pandemic Cubana has had to adapt, putting its dance classes and Latin club nights on hold, yet the lively Latin spirit remains ever present, and they will be ready once again to welcome you with open arms for many more years to come. The show must go on!

Cubana Tapas Bar
Unit 4, Leopold Square,
Sheffield, S1 2JG
0114 2760475
@cubanatapasbar
cubanatapasbar.co.uk

WHY NOT TRY SOME OF THE WORLD'S BEST RUMS, RIGHT HERE IN SHEFFIELD!

Cubana introduces you to some of their prestigious rum collection, voted to be the UK's best by the industry at the Golden Rum Barrel Awards in 2016. We are proud to offer over 250 rums from across the globe, and these are only a handful that we have available. Of course, we have plenty of rums from Cuba and Latin America, but our vast range also extends from as close as Sheffield to as far as India. All our rums are hand-picked for their individual characteristics and historical value.

PLANTATION XO – XO 20TH ANNIVERSARY – BARBADOS

The 20th anniversary Barbados rum from Plantation. A true bartender's favourite, this stunning bottle is only the beginning of the qualities of this rum, and it was first aged in ex-bourbon Caribbean casks then moved to small French oak casks. A smooth and creamy spirit that reveals notes of oak, vanilla and aged cigar tobacco, as well as cocoa and toasted coconut. For a perfect serve, pour a large measure into a glass and light a Romeo y Julieta Churchill cigar.

APPLETON ESTATE – RARE BLEND – JAMAICA

With a population of 2.8 million people, Jamaica is one of the largest Caribbean countries but famed for being very relaxed and carefree – just like its rum! Pungent, powerful and sweet these rums really fire up the taste buds. The rare blend is aged for a minimum of 12 years and this rum has a deep bronze hue. The flavour profile is bold, adding molasses, cocoa and oak to the palate in comparison to the younger expressions. One to savour!

RON ZACAPA – SISTEMA SOLERA CENTENARIO 23 – GUATEMALA

A truly outstanding blend of rums aged between 6 and 23 years. Intense and sweet with well balanced citrus and dried fruits. Bourbon, oak and tannin qualities elevate this rum and add a pleasant density. Elegant, powerful and nothing short of exceptional.

HAVANA CLUB – 1519 – CUBA

The one and only! After doing a 9,000-mile round trip to Havana, we ensured that we were the first bar outside of Cuba to purchase two bottles of this old and rare blend. It proved to be so unique that we couldn't miss the opportunity to showcase it in Sheffield! The ageing process started in the early 1940s, and it first went on sale in Cubana in 2019. Its rarity ensures that we continue to develop our position as one of the country's leading rum venues.

Cubana Tapas Bar
Unit 4, Leopold Square, Sheffield, S1 2JG
0114 2760475
@cubanatapasbar
cubanatapasbar.co.uk

DOMO RESTAURANT

Found on the ground floor of the heritage-listed Eagle Works building in the bustling Kelham Island area, Domo brings a much-welcomed dash of Sardinian spritz to Sheffield.

Since opening in the summer of 2019, Domo restaurant has become a huge hit — not least because of its 5-7pm aperitivo buffet, where punters snack on pizza, bruschetta and olives whilst washing down post-work pints of Menabrea and Aperol Spritz. Its sunbathed courtyard is perfect for alfresco drinking and dining, whilst inside you'll find a spacious restaurant and bar area that is designed in an attractive rustic fashion, adorned with Sardinian masks, handwoven baskets and Mediterranean-style plants.

Owners Sarah Elliott and partner Raffaelle Busceddu have both worked in the restaurant business for a while, but decided to branch out and launch their own venue. Raffaele's well-known uncle and chef Dario owns Rocca 'Ja, a restaurant in Castelsardo — an idyllic little village on the coast of Sardinia. Once the doors to Domo swung open in 2019, the family came to Sheffield to help run the place and install some truly traditional Sardinian character in the eatery.

Even before tucking into the food from one of Domo's inspired menus, it hits just how impressive a place it is. There's the hustle and bustle of a family-run kitchen in one corner — frenetic, passionate and fervent. It's quite something to see that manifested in a plate of hearty food, served with a smile and a "buon appetito", of course. The word Domo means home, and it's clear to see that Sarah and Raffaelle have brought their own version of home to the city of Sheffield, with that unique blend of incredible traditional food served up in an atmosphere akin to a family meal at nonna's place.

If the warm and welcoming feel is the entrée, then the extensive menu at Domo is — quite literally — the *pièce de résistance*. The menu is comprehensive and reflects the wide-ranging flavours enjoyed in authentic Sardinian cuisine. Divided into two sections, 'from the land' and 'from the sea', you can see the importance of sticking to tradition, with key influences taken from a number of the region's areas.

Sarah and Rafaelle's own words sum up this gorgeous restaurant perfectly. "We pride ourselves on serving up food, drink and hospitality you would find in our small town of Castelsardo, Sardinia. We want you to experience the real Sardinian way of life. Whether you need coffee on the go, lunch with colleagues, after-work drinks, feasts with the family, or cocktails at the weekend, we serve up Sardinian tradition all day long. In Castelsardo our door is always open when there's food on the table. We welcome you to our restaurant like we would our home."

Even before tucking into the food from one of Domo's inspired menus, it hits just how impressive a place it is.

Pictures: Ellie Grace

EDO SUSHI

From two school friends kidding about opening a venue twenty years ago, to running one of the most authentic restaurants in the city today. We got in touch with owner Tomo Hasegawa to talk all things sushi and Sheffield.

Can you tell us about the story behind Edo Sushi?

Edo Sushi is brought to you by two good friends, Tomo and Mike. We both grew up in Sheffield and always had a passion for cooking Japanese food. We joked around saying it would be great to open a Japanese place one day. That was about 20 years ago. We opened our first Edo Sushi in 2010. It hasn't been easy and we've been very fortunate to have come across various people along the way that helped us in ways we cannot thank them enough for. The road until now has been a great life and business experience, and we continue to learn each day, from sourcing the best ingredients to how to operate kitchens, run a business and think about expansion effectively. I remember when we first opened, we used to work 16 hours every day. With a spotless kitchen and equipment that was waiting to be used, we waited for the one or two customers that would swing the doors open each day. Things have slightly changed now, but I'm proud and would like to thank the customers still coming to us since the early days!

It's an established name in the restaurant scene in Sheffield now. What's your secret to success?

I wouldn't say there's a secret, nor would I say we're a shining success! I would say, as a small company, we're very fortunate that both myself and Mike love what we do. Loving your job means it's not really work and it brings happiness when things are going in the right direction! We do try to stick to the same ethos: great customer service and good products using high-quality ingredients at affordable prices. It's very easy to say and easier to achieve short-term, but it's the consistency over the years we strive for. Sometimes you need to step out to see what's going on.

Have you got a signature dish? One our readers MUST try for the Edo experience?

The godzilla roll is one of our top sellers. Rightly so, it's so tasty, packed full of flavours and highly nutritious. So far we've had it on every menu at all of the venues we've been fortunate enough to operate and it's still the best seller at our original 'hole in the wall' takeout at High Court.

AVAILABLE ON CITY GRAB

Edo Sushi @ Cutlery Works
73-101 Neepsend Lane,
Neepsend, Sheffield, S3 8AT
cutleryworks.co.uk

Edo Sushi
24-26 High Court Chambers,
Sheffield, S1 2EP
01142 755123 // edosushi.co.uk

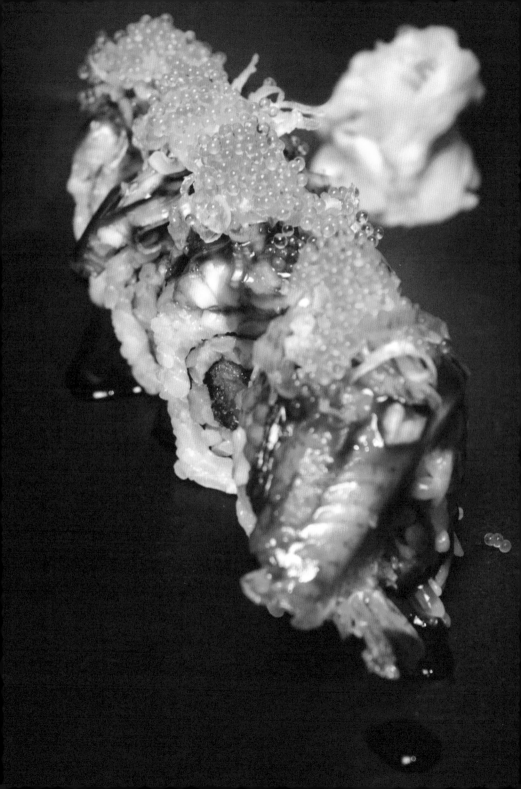

LAVANG

A unique dining experience situated just a stones' throw from some of the city's best nature spots, Lavang brings a decisively modern twist to traditional Indian cuisine.

Nestled in the leafy suburb of Fulwood, Lavang offers a stylish and sophisticated retreat for those seeking high-quality Indian food in a laidback setting. The venue opened in 2017, and it wasn't long before they began to turn heads amongst foodies in the city for their innovative approach.

"We like to have a quality over quantity ethos; the focus is on fresh ingredients with our ever-evolving seasonal menu, brilliant customer service and providing a relaxed ambience for everyone to enjoy. We want to create a unique experience offering dishes people may not have tried in an Indian restaurant before."

The menu serves up indulgent Indian dishes with a fine dining twist, but without the pretentiousness often associated with the latter. Along with the exciting chef specials, their modern ethos is also reflected in the décor – from the clean, crisp interior to the sleek outdoor seating offering customers the option of some al fresco wining and dining.

Location is another key selling point for the restaurant. It is no secret that Fulwood is one of the most sought-after areas in the city, bolstered by some fantastic local pubs and an enviable proximity to the rolling hills of the Peak District. Because of this, Lavang offers the perfect dining destination for those "making a day of it" and tackling the many nearby walking routes and woodland trails.

It's something the owners are particularly proud of, along with a guarantee to go a step further with the food on offer. "The scenery is beautiful around here, and we're really close to local beauty spots like Forge Dam, Whiteley Woods, and of course The Peak District in general, so it's perfectly placed for people looking for a great meal after a day trip."

"There are some nice local places to drink nearby, and we're a short journey from the city centre and Ecclesall Road too. As a venue, we make sure we can provide for any occasion, offering something a bit different to your average Indian restaurant – whether you're eating in, hiring us for a special event or ordering a takeaway."

The venue itself was designed so it could cater for a range of events and functions: business meetings, birthdays, wedding receptions, private hire and more. It's all part of the highly personalised service that sets Lavang apart.

THE LITTLE SNACK BAR

The Little Snack Bar introduced a touch of Taiwan culture to the city back in 2016 when owner Kevin Kuo spotted a small gap in the market for Taiwanese food in Sheffield.

Can you tell us about The Little Snack Bar?

I moved to Sheffield 10 years ago for university and I fell in love with the city and its people. One thing always bugged me – why are there so many Chinese restaurants but no Taiwanese food? No bubble teas? I saw the tiny gap in the market and started the business in July 2016.

Initially I wanted to do two things. First, introduce Taiwanese cuisine. We are famous for bentos, street food from night markets and bubble tea. I choose to do a bit of each.

Secondly, dining culture. Taiwan is a tiny island with way too many people, so you can imagine what life would be like. Everything is competitive and everyone is always in a rush. Instead of having a sandwich, people in Taiwan have bento – a box of rice with meat and veg. Office workers order bentos to be delivered to their office so they can spend the minimum time for lunch and perhaps a bit more for work. I wanted to have a small menu, so you don't stare at hundreds of items and have a choice-phobia. I want to save your time thinking about what to have for lunch or dinner, without sacrificing the joy of eating. We take care of your food, you take care of your time.

What's the secret to a good bubble tea?

I used to think there must be a secret to a good bubble tea until I started doing it, and there isn't! Some people prefer the traditional tea-based bubble tea, in which the quality will solely depend on the tea itself. People who like that appreciate the teas we sell, which are shipped over from Taiwan.

Do you have a signature dish?

Our signature would definitely be the braised pork belly bento. Wherever you go in Taiwan, there is always pork belly rice, it's the most abundant dish. It's a bit like fish and chips to England. We dice the pork belly and braise it for 12 hours with our special soy sauce and herbs. When it is served with rice, the mini diced pork belly just melts in your mouth with the rice, and before you realise it, you have finished the bento already!

AVAILABLE ON CITY GRAB

The Little Snack Bar 104 Devonshire Street, Sheffield, S3 7SF
0114 278 9888 // littlesnackbar.co.uk // littlesnackbar_sheffield

MACPOT

Sisters Emily and Hatty took the leap from cheese and prosecco street food traders to fully fledged restaurant owners in 2020. The restaurant in question, Macpot, is Sheffield's first ever mac and cheese eatery – a natural progression for the 'Frizz and Fromage' sisters. Hatty tells us their story.

Tell us about the background of Macpot and how you came to open the city's first dedicated mac and cheese restaurant.

Back in November 2017, my sister Emily and I were both in jobs which didn't exactly have us leaping out of bed on a Monday morning. So, as a first tentative step to big change, we made a plan to join the street food circuit the following year in our spare time. After a BIG Gin Van vs Food Van debate, the older, bossier sister won out and the first iteration of our business 'Fizz & Fromage' was born. Two years, a name upgrade and a global pandemic later and we're the super proud owners of Macpot, Sheffield's first mac and cheese restaurant. We picked a site on Orchard Terrace in Orchard Square which is undergoing some really exciting regeneration; this plus the central location and massive outside terrace made it too attractive to turn down, despite its slightly daunting size. 2020 hasn't been the start we hoped for, but we've survived so far and hope the fab indy lovers of Sheffield are keen to see us stick around past all the madness.

What is so great about mac and cheese?

Once we had decided to start a food business, mac and cheese was an obvious choice – we were brought up on really good, mum-made versions of home comforts, including that nostalgic favourite. We thought, well, if WE want to see our childhood fave at festivals or on the high street then others will too! Mac and cheese is great for loads of reasons but the simplest for me is cheese! If you ask Em, she'd say because you can put pretty much anything with it and it still tastes good – Macpot's menu centres around this fact. We love our signature Moss Valley pulled pork or veggie toppings with a good old bowl of hot, stretchy mac, but what's really exciting is experimenting with new stuff like brioche burgers loaded with mac and cheese, double-carb brunch Macpots (their signature pot filled with mac and cheese plus toppings) with hash browns, or reimagining of the classic 'steak and chips' with mac and cheese and chimichurri. The possibilities are endless and trust us, they all really work!

What do you love most about Sheffield?

I love that, if you wanted to, you could walk from the old industrial heartland of Kelham right out to the edge of the rolling Peak District in a couple of hours. Our size can be our strength; it gives Sheffield a greener, more village-like feel; you're more likely to bump into people you know out and about. And, as an independent business owner, it's easier to access a community of other business owners. Before we joined the world of street food and restaurants we assumed it would be mega competitive. But it's not; there is a huge sense of camaraderie and being in it together. Perhaps it's because Sheffield is seen as Manchester or Leeds' less cool, younger cousin, but there's definitely a sense of strength in our small numbers.

Macpot, 33, Unit 6 Orchard Square, Sheffield S1 2FB
// info@macpot.co.uk // macpot.co.uk // @MacpotKitchen

THE MOWBRAY

Sally Hubbard, owner at celebrated events space The Mowbray, talks us through how the proudly independent business adapted during a difficult year and plans to see it out with plenty of festive treats.

We're usually an events business hosting weddings, business meetings, conferences, private dining, and celebrations — all of life's good stuff packed with creativity, fun and making beautiful times happen. With our kitchen team we set out to make a creative impact on how event food is presented and have developed a signature style — 'The Feast' — which puts seasonality and 'Mowbray-made' at the heart of all of our menus.

We've been running The Mowbray for three years now, and The Chimney House for fourteen years. Like many other small independent businesses, we've had to totally rethink our plan for 2020 and beyond. If someone had said you'll need to postpone nearly your entire calendar of events for both venues for the year, speed-develop an entire online business, and then open a café (Mow's Coffee), I'd have said no way. But here we are!

Being in and out of lockdown and up and down the tiers system has meant we've been able open for meetings, Petit Weddings, a new style of Supper Clubs, and introduce Kebab Shop and Cocktail Bar as and when we could. The Mowbray is a big space, so we've been able to sit guests in maximum comfort at a fraction of our capacity, but the absence of scale has meant a new community of supporters have turned out en-masse to support us.

At the end of March, we launched The Mowbray at Home, which was all about raising spirits and bringing creative feasting to peoples' homes — food that was reflective of what we'd serve at The Mowbray and The Chimney House.

We're taking The Mowbray at Home through to the end of the year as our last hurrah for 2020 with two ultimate 'at home' menus — Christmas Day Dinner and New Year's Eve — both Feasts to share between two. There's minimum prep needed, so you'll have spectacular feasting on your table in under thirty minutes!

We've also stocked up our Christmas shop with some real treats, including Mow's Christmas Cookies made by The Mowbray Kitchen. It's all designed to give a helping hand this year, with the option to scale your feast up or down regardless of what happens regarding lockdown.

We've put together some Christmas gifts as well. We're gifting some pretty special treats from our little corner of Neepsend; they're presents we hope any Sheffield foodie would be well pleased to receive and are available from The Mowbray online shop.

AVAILABLE ON CITY GRAB

The Mowbray
118 Mowbray St,
Neepsend, Sheffield S3 8EN
0114 276 7885
@themowbray
themowbray.co.uk

THE MOWBRAY

Christmas

AT HOME

RAFTERS

Rafters is a Steel City icon. Guided by the Bosworth brothers, it burst onto the restaurant scene in the 90s, and has long since been the go-to venue for that special occasion.

Good friends Tom and Al bought the restaurant back in 2013 from Marcus Lane, who had previously built Rafters' name for 10 years. After starting out in the industry when they were just 16, the pair were eager to run a business for themselves, committed to bringing the finest European and British cuisine to Sheffield's hungry locals.

The restaurant focuses on the complete package: food, service, and drink. For Tom and Al, a good meal is simply not enough; it requires excellent service and quality drinks as an accompaniment, and their goal is to consistently deliver the best of the best. The kitchen brings a range of seasonal surprises, changing up their dazzling six-course menu in line with the times to add an element of curiosity every time you return. In recent years, the restaurant has been given a makeover, with new solid oak tables made in the area and adorned with Sheffield cutlery from Carrs Silver, fusing the Steel City with the art of fine dining.

Rafters loves to work with local suppliers, and during lockdown a collaboration with Sheffield favourites Locksley Distilling and Bullion Chocolate led to the creation of their newest signature cocktail: The Bullion Chocolate Orange Martini. The key ingredient is a chocolate liqueur, served both in the restaurant and Rafters Neighbourhood Bar. Looking for a boozy treat at the end of a busy day? Below is a quick and easy guide on how you can make your own!

BULLION CHOCOLATE ORANGE MARTINI

Ingredients
50ml Bullion Chocolate Liqueur
25ml Cointreau
12.5ml Dolin Dry Vermouth
1 orange slice
Cocoa powder

Method
Pour all the ingredients into a cocktail shaker over ice and stir for 1 minute.
Rim a glass with orange juice, then dip into the cocoa power.
Strain the cocktail into the glass and serve.

Rafters Restaurant
220 Oakbrook Road, Sheffield, S11 7ED
0114 2304819
@raftersrestaurant
bookings@raftersrestaurant.co.uk
raftersrestaurant.co.uk

SILVERSMITHS

Drawing inspiration from its Yorkshire heritage, Silversmiths produces the finest modern British cuisine, served in a relaxed environment with a dash of fine dining.

Silversmiths Restaurant is in the heart of Sheffield city centre, close to Sheffield Hallam University and the train station, neighbouring the famous Sheffield Crucible and Lyceum theatres – the perfect Sheffield location.

The restaurant was originally founded in 2009 after a transformational visit from Gordon Ramsay as part of the popular TV show 'Kitchen Nightmares'. He taught them to focus on fresh, seasonal Yorkshire produce and in the years following, the restaurant began to receive national acclaim, winning multiple awards along the way.

After a short period of the restaurant falling on hard times, autumn 2019 brought new owners, a gorgeous new refurbishment, a passionate new team and exquisite modern British cuisine. The contemporary interior is warm and inviting, with exposed wood and a slightly industrial feel. You will also see discreet touches around the restaurant with a nod to the past and the long history of the building, which was once a working silversmiths. If you look closely, you can still see the hand-crafted silverware once made in this historic building adorning the walls.

Silversmiths also features a newly decorated private dining suite on the upper floor of the building which can hold up to 14 guests, perfect for any social or corporate event where personal service and that little extra finesse is required.

Everything that comes out of the Silversmiths kitchen has been prepared, preserved, pickled, roasted, baked, mixed and handmade right within its four walls. The kitchen team is led by head chef Ashley Bagshaw, who has brought energy, passion and ability to Silversmiths. You will find classics delivered to perfection alongside much more challenging and unusual dishes that will surprise and delight.

Reflecting over the past year, Silversmiths co-owner Matthew Ray said: "It's incredible how far we've come in just one year. From taking over the business in late 2019, which in recent times had lost its way, to a full renovation – opening our doors for the first time only to be closed down for three months shortly after… It's been challenging to say the least! However, we are so proud of where we are today and the food we are producing is just out of this world."

Silversmiths
111 Arundel Street,
Sheffield S1 2NT
0114 2706160
silversmithsrestaurant.
co.uk

Everything that comes out of the Silversmiths kitchen has been prepared, preserved, pickled, roasted, baked, mixed and handmade right within its four walls.

SILVERSMITHS

> Each dish at Silversmiths is a culinary journey. Using some of the best ingredients, head chef Ashley crafts some of the most unique and flavoursome dishes in the city.

Each dish at Silversmiths is a culinary journey. Using some of the best ingredients, head chef Ashley crafts some of the most unique and flavoursome dishes in the city. Some stand out dishes include the outstanding lamb rump, served with lamb belly, char sui, onion, leek, wasabi, courgetti and a bao bun. Equally as good is the turbot, served with chicken wing, cauliflower, lemon, chicken butter sauce, caper and oyster mushroom. There really is something for everyone!

Also, for the first time, there is a stand-alone vegan and vegetarian menu. Head chef Ashley explains: "We wanted to make our food as accessible to as many people as possible, so we decided to incorporate our own take on vegan and vegetarian fine dining." That certainly is the case with some of the vegan dishes on offer, including the popular falafel with wild garlic, slaw, seaweed, hot sauce and sourdough flatbread. Then there is the vegan tiramisu like you have never seen before, with 85% chocolate, espresso, martini, mango and passionfruit.

In addition to Silversmiths' renowned dinner service, 2020 brought two new additions. Firstly, their Sunday Lunch, which is fast becoming the city's favourite Sunday roast location. Using the finest, locally sourced, 32-day dry-aged beef or roast loin of pork, all served with a huge Yorkshire pudding and seasonal veg, it really is something to behold. It's also great value too, with 3 courses for only £25.

There's also the new Bottomless Brunch menu. Definitely not your standard Bottomless Brunch, all the menu items have that extra special Silversmiths twist. From the eggs Benedict which uses the finest wagyu bacon for extra depth and richness, to the finest lobster rolls you will find, using fresh lobster caught off the Cornish coast only 24 hours before service. Just as exciting, all the drinks on offer are available to mix and match. Choose from a selection of hand-crafted cocktails, classic Prosecco or ice cold beers. No need to stick to one drink, as you can try them all! Silversmiths bottomless brunch is fast gaining a reputation as being Sheffield's premium brunch establishment, perfect for spending quality time with friends and loved ones.

Silversmiths is the perfect choice for that post-lockdown treat. They have all the correct social distancing measures in place, including hand sanitation stations throughout and social distancing screens. All staff members are required to regularly wash their hands, wear gloves and a face mask during service. They have set up the ideal environment for you to feel safe and comfortable when choosing to dine in their company.

Silversmiths
111 Arundel Street,
Sheffield S1 2NT
0114 2706160
silversmithsrestaurant.
co.uk

STREET FOOD CHEF

Abi and Richard Golland, founders of the ever-popular Street Food Chef, tell us what they love about street food, Sheffield and being part of a local community that's seen them through ten years of tasty burritos and wraps...

Street Food Chef feels like a real Sheffield institution these days. Where did it all start?

Well, Street Food Chef is actually ten years old, as of May 2020, so we have been around a while! It began with a street food trailer, and Richard and I spent that first year travelling all over the country. We went everywhere: Glasgow, Cardiff, London, and of course Sheffield, where we did Peace in the Park, the food festivals and Tramlines. The rest is history, as they say!

So what drew you to street food initially?

We both love the theatre of street food and the way it involves direct interaction with your customers. Having ran a restaurant before, Richard was keen to move away from bricks and mortar initially, and our personal values about food leaned towards doing a smaller thing really well with a limited menu, so we could offer great quality, chef-cooked food at reasonable prices.

Describe the ethos of your business; what's most important to you both?

I'd say we have four main 'pillars' at Street Food Chef that are equally important. Firstly, the food is the star of the show. We make everything ourselves so it's all fresh and cooked from scratch. Our customers' experiences, whether with delivery, takeaway or eating in, are always a priority too: we want them to love the interaction and the environment as much as we do. Lastly, we love working with local suppliers where possible. Giving back to the community and economy is key because we wouldn't be where we are today if Sheffield hadn't got behind us.

What do you love most about being based in Sheffield?

I think Sheffield is naturally a very entrepreneurial city, and street food really suits it: they're both honest, straightforward, there's no messing about. Over the last ten years we've seen massive changes in the city's street food scene; it's grown and developed so much and people are far more comfortable trying new things which is great for us. It's a very supportive place too and continues to be a brilliant home for Street Food Chef.

AVAILABLE ON CITY GRAB

Street Food Chef Sharrow Vale
376 Sharrow Vale Road, Sheffield S11 2ZP
0114 327 4778
arundel@streetfoodchef.co.uk
sharrow@streetfoodchef.co.uk

Street Food Chef
90 Arundel Street, Sheffield S1 4RE
0114 275 2390
arundel@streetfoodchef.co.uk
streetfoodchef.co.uk

TRUE NORTH BREW CO.

**From posters and print to reinventing pubs with
Kane Yeardley, Managing Director**

Can you start by telling us a bit about the True North story and how you came to do what you do?

I went to Leicester Poly, now De Montfort University, to study surveying. There I started a vintage clothing business, club promoting, and dealing in posters and prints. When I left, I decided I didn't really want to be a surveyor and I found posters and prints interesting. If anything sold really well you could always reprint it. It was a lot easier than sourcing second hand clothes, dealing with nightclub owners, and unreliable DJs and bouncers. As the business grew, I travelled quite a bit to find new distributors: Amsterdam, Berlin, Barcelona, New York, Prague etc. What I saw in these cities is they had a café bar culture which Sheffield didn't have. You have to remember 30 years ago the only way for somebody to get a new license was if they bought it from a pub that was being knocked down. After I opened the Forum as a restaurant/café/gallery I decided I wanted to get it fully licensed and open it late. I managed to get it through court. At the same time, I'd been going down to London and I saw this model where pubs had a quirky design, shabby chic, they would do good food, good cocktails and later on in the evening you'd have a DJ till 3am. In Islington there was the Embassy and Keston Lodge, there were DJs such as Richard Fearless, Death in Vegas, and James Murphy (LCD Soundsystem). I thought "hello", this could work in Broomhill (The York) and Abbeydale Road (The Broadfield). But before those, I saw the Elbow Rooms, a cool pool hall, which inspired me to do The Common Room. After these I got the bug for reinventing pubs and seeing people have a good time going out to those pubs again.

How has 2020 impacted True North venues?

It's been very tough because our teams and I are so used to seeing all our venues buzzing and full of life. I felt like I had nothing better to do than go round and check that there weren't any leaks or break-ins. This time round, we're near to completing some projects regarding getting planning permission and building quotes. We've added a terrace to The Punch Bowl, Crookes, doubling the size of the outside area, and we're working on a new concept to develop The Old Grindstone in Crookes next year. At The Milton Arms, Elsecar, we plan to enlarge the garden and put in another function room/conservatory. We are also making our outside areas more comfortable in most of our venues by sourcing marquees with heating and lighting, plus the True North décor our customers know.

What have you and your staff been doing to keep up morale and support one another during this time?

We have a staff newsletter put together by Isla Macaskill from The York. It is full of shoutouts to team members, funny stories, recipes and I make a playlist every month to be included, not to

everyone's taste maybe but some good progressive house tracks for when we're all stuck in the house. "One nation under a roof". We have kept in touch with everyone via Microsoft Teams and have regular online socials. It is nice to see everyone's faces. We have launched takeaway in our venues which is not an easy feat but has given sites a focus and an opportunity to keep in touch with our customers and their colleagues.

Sheffield is all about supporting local – what can the people of Sheffield do to support True North venues during these times?

When we reopen, come and visit us and meet your friends here. We can't wait to see you. You can support us now by trying out our takeaway service, which is also click and collect. The Broadfield have their famous pies on offer and you can create the True North experience at home. We've been amazed by the demand for Sunday roasts, especially from The Waggon & Horses, it's probably their famous gravy.

There are plenty of options available for Christmas gifts for drinks lovers from the True North store. Are you working on any new beers/gins/spirits, be it new flavours or new products entirely?

This year we are opening a gin shop in the Forum Shops where you can come and pick up gift sets, all of our gins and ask any questions from our gin experts. All our products are also available to buy online (truenorthbrewco.uk/store), either for delivery or collection from the Forum Shops. Dean Hollingworth, our head brewer, has a 6% Double IPA on keg and a 6% Dark Ruby Mild Cask lined up for the festive period. We have also created a new flavour of Leeds Gin – Mulled Nordic Berries. Stones Bitter will be back and I'm hoping it will go down great. Also, we've just launched a virtual gin tasting masterclass, led by our head curator, Tom Hay-Owens, that you can do with your friends, family and colleagues online from the comfort of your own home.

TOP PICKS FOR A PROPER GOOD TIME IN SHEFFIELD

True North Brew Co. is a leading independent pub, bar and restaurant group with 12 venues across South Yorkshire and Derbyshire. Known for delivering excellent eating and drinking experiences as well as producing Sheffield Dry Gin, Leeds Gin, True North Beer, Sheffield Vodka and coffee, they know a thing or two about a good old knees-up.

In Sheffield, three sought-after venues are situated in the popular Devonshire Quarter and include Forum Kitchen + Bar, The Common Room, and The Old House. The iconic Riverside Kelham is based just outside the city centre in the upcoming area of Kelham Island. Taking you directly out of the city and into the surrounding suburbs of Broomhill and Crookes are The York and The Punch Bowl, whilst Sheffield's most illustrious venues, The Broadfield and The Waggon and Horses are within walking distance of each other in the residential ward of Ecclesall. Make your way out of Sheffield and you'll find rustic favourites, The British Oak in Mosborough and The Blue Stoops in Dronfield. To complete the portfolio, Barnsley is home to The Crown and Anchor and The Milton Arms. Sometimes it's hard to decide what to do first when you want to have a proper good time in Sheffield, purely because there is so much choice and that's why True North's Marketing Manager, Krissie Petfield has put together a list of recommendations for you:

Eat award-winning pies

If there's one thing that True North pubs are known for, it's a love of great food! Anyone that has visited will know all about our delicious, award-winning pies. Whether you're a fan of the classic steak pie, a one-off special that uses the best locally-sourced ingredients, or you prefer an animal-friendly alternative, you'll have plenty to choose from.

Play pool and watch sports at the same time!

An all-out sports bar is sure to satisfy everyone in your group and especially one with an awesome vegan food menu, 11 full size American pool tables, ping pong and over 50 giant TV screens showing the latest sporting events all day, every day (just about!). The Common Room is Sheffield's only two floor city centre sports bar.

Go bottomless for brunch

Is there a better way to spend 90 minutes than by having a booze-soaked feast to close the week on a high? Book a Bottomless Mimosa, Prosecco or Heineken Brunch between Thursday and Sunday and choose from any of our delicious brunch items to accompany... After all, what's the point of eggs Benedict without unlimited mimosas, anyway?

Make your own bottle of gin

Sheffield Dry Gin was the first gin to be distilled and bottled in Sheffield in over 100 years. Develop your own bespoke recipe at the Sheffield School of Gin, where you will also learn all about the history of gin, develop a deeper understanding of botanicals and become an expert in the distillation of gin. A great experience for a special occasion.

MOORLAND RAMBLE COCKTAIL

Hints of dark berries to the fore, blackberry and cranberry with hints of blueberry coming through on the finish.

Moorland Berries is distilled blending hand-picked blueberries, cranberries and blackberries, found naturally on Sheffield's surrounding moors and heathlands.

Ingredients
5 dried blueberries
50ml Sheffield Dry Gin Moorland Berries
25ml gomme
15ml freshly squeezed lemon juice
10ml crème de mûre

Method
Soak the dried blueberries overnight in 50ml of Sheffield Dry Gin Moorland Berries. Add the gin, gomme, and lemon juice to a Boston shaker filled with ice. Shake and strain into a lowball glass filled with ice.
Float the crème de mûre over the top and garnish with the gin-soaked blueberries.

PORK, FENNEL AND CIDER SAUSAGE

Ingredients
800g lean pork shoulder
400g pork belly, skin removed
20g salt
2 tbsp fennel seeds
115ml good cold cider
1 tbsp freshly ground pepper
Edible sausage casing

Method
Roughly chop the shoulder and the belly. Grind the meat using a 0.5cm diameter grinder. Put the ground meat in a bowl. Add the salt, cider, fennel seeds and ground pepper and knead well until the liquid has been well absorbed, keeping everything cool. Stuff the sausage into the casing, avoid any air bubbles and tie it off with a bubble knot. Let the sausages rest in the fridge overnight before cooking. Grill gently and prick with a cocktail stick if required.

AVAILABLE ON CITY GRAB

True North Brew Co.
7 Eldon St,
Sheffield S1 4GX
@truenorthbrewco
truenorthbrewco.uk

Q+A WITH DEAN HOLLINGWORTH, HEAD BREWER

You've been with True North for a while now. What's been your favourite brew so far?

I've been fortunate to experiment with new ideas and collaborate with other breweries over the years and even with artist Phlegm to produce a 6% stout for his exhibition 'Mausoleum of the Giants'. But my favourite is definitely bringing Stones best bitter back to Sheffield. We used a traditional cask recipe with Challenger and Goldings hops and the original Stones yeast strain, kindly given to us by Molson Coors. I was even more honoured and elated when I met two of the last people to brew Stones at Cannon Brewery and they gave our brew the thumbs up.

What sets True North beers apart do you think?

Our beer production is predominantly to supply the True North venues which means that we try to appeal to everyone and have a good standard core range – a blonde, a best bitter, a pale and a pilsner – as well as some of the more exciting styles like NEIPAs.

Let's talk gin. The Sheffield Dry Gin core range has five very different flavours. How do you decide what makes the cut?

We incorporate interesting and seasonal ingredients and only use whole fruit so the end result has to be a flavour that distills well, like raspberries for instance. In May 2020, we added Strawberry and Black Pepper to the lineup after it was so well received by our customers. The core range also includes Sheffield Dry Gin Original, Raspberry and Pomegranate, Moorland Berries and Marmalade.

Sheffield Dry Gin is the first gin to be distilled and bottled in Sheffield in over 100 years. What's been the biggest moment of success since then?

We have had great success and growth year on year with Sheffield Dry Gin enabling us to grow the range from one to five core flavours, as well as multiple special releases and collaborations with the likes of Sheffield's Kid Acne. Our gin has even been enjoyed as far away as Sydney! One of our biggest successes has been opening a site in Leeds to distill Leeds Gin, which has a core range of Original Dry, Strawberry and Raspberry, Apple and Blackberry and Parma Violet. It's stocked nationally by Harvey Nichols, which is a great achievement, and for Christmas we've launched a Mulled Nordic Berries flavour.

To complete the produce collection, you also make Sheffield Vodka and roast your own coffee. Can you tell us a bit more about this?

Sheffield Vodka is double distilled using 100% wheat grain spirit, giving it a lovely buttery smooth aftertaste, alongside spice from the addition of cracked black pepper, and a nice fresh crisp aroma from vapour infused with hand-cut lemon peel.

We're passionate about great coffee. We want to make sure that when you step inside one of our venues you can always get a quality cup of coffee. To maintain consistency and high quality, we work with trusted suppliers to ethically source the finest Arabica beans that are grown by Brazilian and Guatemalan farmers using traditional methods. We then roast the beans in house to create a unique taste and lock in all of the flavour.

URBAN CHOOLA

Taking pride in being the No.1 Indian restaurant in Sheffield on TripAdvisor, Urban Choola is a firm favourite and certainly not one to be missed. With traditional dishes being served in an up-market style, it's easy to see why the city just can't get enough of their rich, spicy flavours.

Their menu is designed in line with Dastaan Indian restaurant, a multi-award-winning Michelin recommended venue, and they share ownership of both Dastaan and Urban Choola. The owner, Anurag Singh, has a passion for creating authentic Indian cuisine with a contemporary twist. Plating up the dishes with a strong focus on presentation and finer dining is of the utmost importance to him; India has an endless array of dishes and spices ready to be respected and showcased with the same beauty as their taste.

He opened Urban Choola in 2012 to immediate success. Since then has adapted and changed the menu yearly, introducing some new dishes to intrigue of the customer, whilst also keeping some old, firm favourites that locals hungrily come back for. The restaurant flourishes day in day out, with diners falling in love with their high-end approach to Indian dining.

Star dishes range from duck and chicken seekh to a classic chicken tikka, as well as creative vegetarian options and inspired vegan dishes such as beetroot tikki and tandoori broccoli, which really tickle the taste buds. The drinks menu is equally tasty, with a full bar including both traditional and Indian-style cocktails. The Thandai cocktail is an indulgent combination of vodka, amaretto, cream and saffron, perfectly complementing the curries and creating an explosive flavour palate.

Sourcing their produce as locally and sustainably as possible is really important to Anurag: "We supply meat and veg locally as much as we can and also import spices as well as other produce from sustainable sources in India: our suppliers know exactly which Indian farms they are coming from. We keep the menu seasonal and change it as regularly as possible so there is something new to try for everyone".

With Urban Choola always looking to expand and grow, in recent years they have catered for events such as weddings and birthdays, as well as providing menus for Diwali and Christmas. They have become a beloved and treasured culinary experience in Sheffield, embracing all things deliciously and authentically Indian with a nod to modern city life.

URBAN PIZZA CO.

Taking a little inspiration from their travels across the globe, Urban Pizza Co. impressively manages to offer something unique and special to the pizza industry.

Found in the vibrant hub of Steelyard in Kelham Island, this popular pizzeria is part of the Urban Entertainment group, which specialise in events including outdoor and drive-in cinema evenings both in the UK and the Middle East. They make pizzas using only the finest ingredients to ensure everything on their menu is as tasty as it looks, and their passion, love and attention to detail really is reflected in the food they produce.

Being focused on bringing quality pizzas to hungry Sheffielders, they take pride in being a close-knit team. "Having the right people and balance around you is the most important aspect in any business," Director Michael Hayes tells us. "Our team consists of amazing chefs that allow us to create truly delicious and unique pizzas; we can experiment knowing that our ingredients are something you would expect in the finest high-end restaurants."

These pizzas certainly stand out from the crowd. The specials menu includes their mouth-watering Chicken Tikka pizza, which consists of tandoori marinated chicken on a masala base, fior di latte mozzarella and fresh garnish. Other favourites are the El Mariachi, which is a Mexican-inspired pizza, Burrata with their in-house walnut pesto and the Nduja special, which is a sweet and spicy creation accompanied by their in-house dipping sauce (a secret recipe of course!). They also offer many vegetarian, vegan and gluten-free options throughout their menu, including the zesty Vegan Greek which is always a popular choice for customers, and all of the vegetarian pizzas can be made vegan.

The pizzeria itself is unique to the eye; inspired by the quirkiness of Kelham Island, they are proud to be made entirely from shipping containers, and this cool architecture is designed in a way that reflects their urban brand, experimental menu and the space they sit in at Steelyard. The area is also home to an assortment of many other unique and independent businesses from restaurants to shops, redefining the conventions of food and retail platforms and connecting people to Sheffield's industrial culture.

Their plans are to roll this concept out in the UK and the UAE, with interest already from developments further afield and possible franchises and concessions, so we really are expecting to see even bigger things from the company in the future.

AVAILABLE ON CITY GRAB

Urban Pizza Co
Unit 01, Steelyard
Kelham, Bardwell Road,
Sheffield, S3 8AS
0114 2760475
@urbanpizzaco1
urbanpizzaco.co.uk

RESTAURANTS

Whether you're looking for sizzling street food or a modern approach to fine dining, here are some of the best foodie hangouts in Sheffield.

Church – Temple of Fun // templeof.fun

This exciting 'barcade' venture from Sheffield lad and Bring Me The Horizon singer Oli Sykes is a bit of everything, making it a solid choice for a wide variety of worshipping purposes. Visitors can expect tasty vegan snap, live events, retro arcade machines, bar games, and a lively night out all wrapped up in a historic riverside warehouse – once a large toolmaking factory – situated just outside of Kelham Island.

Pom // pomkitchen.co.uk

"Rainbow food" is all the rage on Insta these days, and Pom's multi-coloured meals are certainly photo-friendly. They have a toast bar, daily hot and cold meals and a fabulous range of desserts, including frozen coconut served in half a coconut. This is one to shake up your diet, and your social media feed.

Napoli Centro // napolicentro.co.uk

Authentic wood-fired Neapolitan pizza and street food snacks, what more could you ask of a pizza place? Napoli Centro has a fantastic rep in the city, boasting a top 5 TripAdvisor rating for restaurants across Sheffield.

The Bhaji Shop // thebhajishop.co.uk

With a deli on Abbeydale Road and the main kitchen on Chesterfield Road, this much-loved and longstanding business is home to infamous bhajis and delicious Indian-style food from wraps to takeaway curries. Colourful, fresh and always served with a smile!

La Mama // lamamalatin.co.uk

Visit La Mama for an authentic taste of Latin America in the popular Abbeydale Road area. Enjoy delicious tapas at home or in the restaurant alongside speciality wines, beers and cocktails. The owners pride themselves on creating a true Latino atmosphere and traditional food from Chile and Spain.

Nether Edge Pizza // netheredgepizza.com

From humble beginnings with a single mobile oven, this well-established venture now pops up at foodie events all over the city. There are now two pizzerias, one on Abbeydale Road and one in Kelham Island, turning out beautiful wood-fired pizzas as well as three mobile ovens working at weddings, private parties and more.

VorV // vorvsheffield.co.uk

Coffee house by day, restaurant by night, and everything is vegetarian or vegan: this characterful spot in Kelham Island has something for everyone. There's a big emphasis on sustainability and ethical sourcing for all their food, drink and even furniture so you can enjoy a planet-friendly evening out or daytime pit-stop.

Porter Pizza Company // porterpizza.co.uk

The Italian-inspired pizzas at Porter's small but perfectly formed venue on Sharrow Vale Road are almost works of art. The dough is made daily and proved overnight, hand-stretched, topped with authentic ingredients and wood-fired the traditional way for maximum flavour and a proper crust. You can order delivery but it's worth the trip for the freshest pizza possible.

Bench // facebook.com/benchsheffield
Bench is a neighbourhood hangout with communal bistro-style dining serving seasonal dishes alongside cocktails, natural wine and beer. It's also a shop selling those same natural wines and ready-to-drink cocktails alongside charcuterie, for the perfect date night in. New on the scene but already making a big name for themselves amongst Sheffield's independents.

Cutlery Works // cutleryworks.co.uk
The largest foodhall in the north of England serving a range of cuisines from fresh sushi to Indian street food. Spread across two floors, Cutlery Works is a popular social destination for a bite to eat or a night out with pals. Special events such as bottomless brunches and wine-tastings regularly take place, there's a popular craft beer bar as well as a nicely refined section for cocktails, and during the day it's popular for the more indulgent types of work lunches.

Kommune // kommune.co.uk
Situated in the up-and-coming Castlegate area of the city, this sleek social hub opened in 2019 and is home to variety of food traders serving throughout the day and into the evening. There's also an art gallery, retail traders and a well-stocked bar to keep you entertained.

Dyson Place // dysonplace.co.uk
Bringing together an exciting combination of independents and modern living space in an inviting courtyard setting, the Dyson Place development is a popular hangout spot for shoppers and foodies. A number of businesses have taken up residence since its 2020 opening including Vietnamese kitchen Năm Sông and innovative small plates specialists Tonco have been a popular draw, you'll also find Olive and Joy serving up vegan treats and coffee, children's clothing label Bear & Babe, quirky interior and lighting shop Inco, eco-friendly hair salon The Nook, integrative women's health clinic Life + Lemons, popular barbers Rapscallions, and recent foodie addition Pellizco.

La Baracca // labaraccasheffield.business.site
A small family-run Italian restaurant in the heart of the Antiques Quarter of Sheffield on Abbeydale Road. Saverio, owner and chef, has lived in the city for over 30 years and this isn't his first culinary enterprise. He ran Dino's on London Road with his wife Lorraine for 10 years before moving back to Italy for a short while. The style is definitely rustic and La Baracca serves up real home-cooked comfort food in a friendly atmosphere.

Greedy Greek Deli // greedygreekdeli.co.uk
A family-run business which has been serving up the tastiest Greek cuisine to hungry Sheffielders since 2003. A street food favourite situated on Sharrow Vale Road, the secret to their longevity is simple: fresh, authentic food served with a smile. Keep an eye out for the Greedy Greek van at any local events too!

PUBS + BARS

BARROWBOY

Barrowboy began the way most ideas begin — over a beer. Owners Morgan Davies and Charlie Marks had discussed it for years and it had taken on many iterations and many names...

"We always wanted to do something in Sheffield," says Charlie. "We started seriously looking at Meersbrook, Netheredge and Abbeydale but things kept getting in the way. It wasn't the right time." When 453 came up, the boys decided it was now or never. The name Barrowboy was a nod to the hundred-year history the venue had of being a grocery store. "The old ideas went out the window. We decided to just make the bar we wanted to go to. Something for the neighbourhood, where everyone knows your name," Morgan says, grinning.

They contacted Deckards (then a bao bun street food outlet, now permanent residents at the bar) over Instagram, started throwing together "rag-tag" designs, gutted the place, employed Rocket Design, went through the many legalities and got together a team, in what "felt like a whirlwind." The team was also very important to them, as they wanted Barrowboy to be friendly and welcoming, as well as serving great drinks.

The two general managers they've employed have both played vital roles in the bar's success. The current manager, Pete, has become part of the furniture on Abbeydale Road. "He spends all our money on making the place better," Morgan says. "The place has a brilliant vibe and that's created by Pete and the team. It's a pleasure to be there."

The Barrowboy team let Deckards focus on the food while they focus on the atmosphere, drinks and events. There's a mouth-watering cocktail menu, draught beers, craft beers and a delicious selection of wines. Pre-Covid, Friday and Saturday nights were lively affairs, with dancing and partying heavily encouraged and a DJ in the corner. "We can't wait to get back to that," says Pete. "People need to dance."

Barrowboy has also hosted live music sessions and started a monthly comedy night which was very popular. It's something the team want to get back to, once the world has returned to some normality. "We can't wait," Morgan says. "Abbeydale Road is amazing now. Gravel Pit, Bragazzi's, Turner's, Dead Donkey, Two Thirds and all the rest of us. Shops, bars, restaurants: there's some of the best that Sheffield has to offer right here and it's all independent. Long may it continue."

Barrowboy
453 Abbeydale Road,
Nether Edge,
Sheffield S7 1FS
0114 220 4530
@barrowboybar

DECKARDS

Declan Stafford, co-owner and chef at bao bun hotspot Deckards, discusses how it all started and their journey so far...

When did you first start serving bao buns, and why did you choose to focus on them?

I first discovered bao on my travels through Australia and Thailand. When I came back to the UK in 2017, not many places were offering them so my friend Nico and I came up with the concept of Deckards. We started doing pop-ups and then residencies, getting a following by word of mouth until our first real breakthrough with Bustler Market in Derby, then Peddler in Sheffield. As for why we chose them, a bao bun is basically a sandwich but way more interesting: a perfect vessel for flavours that you can keep experimenting with. They're brilliant!

How did Barrowboy come into the picture?

They approached us with the idea of setting up permanently in the bar's kitchen, and we snapped up the opportunity. We moved in during the summer of 2018, and won Best Street Food at the Exposed Awards in our first year there, which we're very proud of. Beer and bao has proved a popular combo; I think our food really lends itself to Barrowboy's whole experience. We like to keep our menu small to keep the quality up, and there's all sorts of references to pop culture (Nico and I are massive nerds) which adds to the sense of fun.

Have things changed much since then?

We've seen Abbeydale Road become much more of a destination since our arrival. There's a really strong independent scene here which is fantastic, and a feeling of community: everyone supports each other. Forge Bakehouse used to make our burger buns, Danny and co at Gravel Pit have always been good to us, and we're surrounded by other amazing bars and restaurants... Deckards has almost grown with the area in that sense.

What's next for Deckards?

We're keen to do more pop-ups alongside our regular home; in 2020 we worked with Ambulo to do a one-off evening of refined small plates, and collaborating with the chefs was really enjoyable. It's a great dynamic and I find the food industry so creative, especially when you're bouncing ideas off each other. We also opened in Leicester at Lane7 and started a 'baodega' for lockdown 2.0 which is a kind of urban grocery: everything from ready-made plain bao buns to homemade sauces, probably toilet roll and our very own digital cook book!

AVAILABLE ON CITY GRAB

Deckards
453 Abbeydale Road, Nether Edge, Sheffield S7 1FS
Instagram @deckardsfood
deckardsfood@outlook.com

HOP HIDEOUT

Founded by ale aficionado Jules Gray in 2013, Hop Hideout is home to an increasingly eclectic selection of craft beers, ciders and wines...

Hop Hideout is an award-winning speciality beer shop and tasting room, founded in 2013 as a 'labour of beery love' by Jules Gray. A beer professional, Jules was already passionate about craft beer; blogging regularly about the subject for Exposed Magazine whilst working at a brewery before deciding to launch her own independent beery business.

The business originally started in the back of an antiques centre on Abbeydale Road in Sheffield's Antiques Quarter before moving into a nearby cafe space and then onto its new food hall home at Kommune (on the site of the Grade II listed former Co-Op building) in the city centre in 2019. One of the first 'drink in' beer shops in the UK, they have 200+ chilled beers available to browse, enjoy there and then or takeaway – including four fresh rotating draught taps.

In 2020 they launched a dedicated tap, focusing on showcasing neighbouring Attercliffe brewery, Saint Mars of the Desert, which means you can enjoy a stroll along the canal on a summer's day between Hop Hideout and the brewery taproom, stopping at The Dorothy Pax along the way if you so wish.

Owner Jules has a particular penchant for wild ales, funky beers, natural wines and farmhouse cider, and loves nothing more than helping you find something you love to drink. And just as importantly, there's a genuine sense of community around the shop with regular events such as Meet the Brewers and beer and food matched tasting sessions while they also host the monthly Sheffield chapter of the global Mikkeller Running Club.

Passionate about Sheffield, good causes, and making beer a welcoming space for everyone, Jules is also founder and organiser of annual city-wide beer event Sheffield Beer Week and independent craft beer festival Indie Beer Feast.

With a curated range of quality ciders nestled in alongside natural wines and a craft beer offering from around the world, Hop Hideout has picked up accolades such as RateBeer Best Bottleshop in South Yorkshire (2019).

Hop Hideout
Unit 11, Kommune,
1-13 Angel Street,
Sheffield S3 8LN

Photos: Mark Newton

PIÑA

A few years ago, Joe Cribley embarked on the trip of a lifetime around Mexico with a concise to-do list: eat tacos and drink mezcal.

Vibrant bar and restaurant piña has brought a passion for real Mexican food and drink to Kelham Island. It all started with a journey that took Joe, the owner and founder, from Jalisco and Michoacán to Oaxaca and Mexico City, where he soon fell in love with the people, the culture and above all the cuisine. The trip was financed by a tequila company so although it was drinks-led initially, Joe stayed on for another week to learn about not only the country's distilleries but also its food, which he describes as "an exciting and eye-opening" experience.

By creating piña, Joe and his family have chosen a deliberate take on Mexican cuisine - focusing on tacos and tequila - to make it as accessible yet authentic as possible. The bar and restaurant offers proper tacos in an appropriate setting, encouraging customers to eat them as they should be eaten: with your hands! The traditional fish tacos are hugely popular; battered white fish served with pico de gallo, pickled cabbage and mayo crema in a corn tortilla, creating an explosion of vibrant, fresh flavours.

The small but carefully curated cocktail list accompanies the taco menu, designed to introduce tequila and mezcal to the people of Sheffield. Joe hopes to enlighten people who think they hate tequila, having only drunk poor quality versions: unlike most varieties sold in the UK, at piña it's all 100% agave-based and of the highest quality. "It's nice to know that we've become the place to get good tequila and mezcal in Sheffield, and people know what a good margarita tastes like now," says Joe.

The freshly made food and drinks, warm colours against exposed brickwork and relaxed ambience welcome everyone in at piña. Fusing the charm of their setting, an old warehouse in Sheffield's former industrial quarter, with the brightness of Mexican culture and cuisine has created a beautifully unique haven in the heart of the city.

As Kelham Island has changed over the years, piña has also adapted and evolved to find its niche. The bar and restaurant has become a much-loved culinary experience in Sheffield, thanks to its truly independent spirit. Having previously worked at The Great Gatsby and other hospitality hotspots around the city, Joe is proud to be part of a network of such businesses, all battling the pandemic amidst the strength of community spirit which has really been demonstrated during these tough times.

piña
3 Harvest Lane,
Neepsend,
Sheffield S3 8EF
info@barpina.co.uk
Instagram @ pina.
sheffield

HOW TO MAKE HOMEMADE TORTILLAS

Preparation time: 30 minutes | Cooking time: 3-4 minutes per tortilla | Makes about 12-15

Equipment
1 tortilla press
1 non-stick frying pan or flat griddle
1 mixing bowl
1 weighing scale
1 measuring jug
Greaseproof paper

Ingredients
200g masa harina corn flour
250-300ml water
Salt
Vegetable oil

Before using your tortilla press, you'll need to cut your greaseproof paper down to size so that you have square sheets that fit nicely between the two plates of the tortilla press.

Combine the corn flour with a pinch of salt in a large mixing-bowl and add the water bit by bit, mixing with your hands, until it becomes a 'playdough' like consistency. Avoid adding too much water, as this will create too wet a dough. It should remain malleable. Roll balls of tortilla dough using your palms, each weighing 30 to 35g, or slightly smaller than a golf ball if you don't have scales, and place back into the bowl. Once you've rolled the lot, place a clean, slightly damp tea towel over the bowl to prevent the dough from drying out.

Open your tortilla press and position one piece of greaseproof paper on the bottom plate. Place one ball of dough in the centre and gently flatten the ball with your hand. Place a second piece of greaseproof over the dough and close the tortilla press. Gently apply pressure using the arm of the tortilla press to spread the tortilla dough out evenly. Quick tip: two gentle presses is better than one firm press. Open the press, flip or rotate the dough and repeat. If it's not right, just re-roll the dough and try again!

Heat a non-stick frying pan or griddle to about 260°c. Before you start cooking, wet a piece of kitchen roll with a small amount of vegetable oil and give the pan's surface a quick wipe. This can be done between cooking each tortilla and will help prevent sticking.

Place the pressed tortilla dough in the centre of your heated pan and cook for approximately 1 minute. Using a spatula or slice, test the edges of the tortilla before flipping to cook for a further 2 to 3 minutes on the second side, until you start to see little golden and light brown markings. Once cooked, wrap in a clean kitchen towel to keep warm.

Should you need to reheat your tortillas just before serving, you can either flash fry them in the pan or wrap them in foil and throw them in oven for 10 minutes at 160-180°c. Once hot, keep them wrapped in the tea towel and serve them in their rightful place, the centre of the table!

piña
3 Harvest Lane,
Neepsend,
Sheffield S3 8EF
info@barpina.co.uk
Instagram @ pina.
sheffield

PUBLIC

From pizza and ping-pong to high-end cocktails and late-night merrymaking, these three bars from The Rockingham Group have all of the bases covered.

Occupying the former gents' toilet below the Grade I-listed Victorian town hall, Public is a tiny haven of fine drinks and delicious food, or, as it was once described, 'A Wes Anderson train carriage crowbarred into an old bog'. Since 2017, they've been serving the Sheffield community their creations and along the way have won accolades such as Observer's Best Place to Drink in the UK, Class Awards – Best Bar Food in the UK and Exposed Awards Best New Bar in 2018 and Best Bar in 2019.

The cocktails are an extension of the bar, tethered to its location, this city, seasonality, and its collaborators. They develop their drinks primarily to be delicious, but also try and push the boundaries of where flavour can be taken and tell a story with every cocktail.

From the inception of Public, they've excelled the standard of food that can be achieved from a ridiculously small kitchen; be that homemade pasta, seasonal small plates or the famed toastie, the food and drink works in tandem and combines to give people an experience that is uniquely Public.

With super passionate staff, from the whisky nerd to the wine geek, their talented team enables this subterranean gem to give you the things you love and the things you might not know you love!

Photography by India Hobson.

PUBLIC
23-55 Surrey St, Sheffield
S1 2LG
@P_U_B_L_I_C_
publicpublic.co.uk

GATSBY

Ten years in the game and still going strong… just! Despite a very close brush with death at the beginning of lockdown due to the usual myopia of a pubco landlord, the decade-old boozer on the corner of Division Street and Rockingham Street is set to rise, phoenix-like, from the ashes of 2020.

The Gatsby is a total chameleon. A civilised after-work pint? A bangin' burrito from the (returning) Shy Boy Cantina? Or a completely uncivilised 3am rager on a Saturday night? We've done all these things and more within the cosy confines of this much-loved place.

With the challenges facing city centres and the homogenisation of the high streets, places like The Great Gatsby feel more vital than ever and we look forward to ten more years of hustle from this pocket rocket of a pub!

Photography by India Hobson.

Gatsby
73-75 Division St, Sheffield S1 4GE
@gatsbysheffield
thegatsbybar.co.uk

PICTURE HOUSE SOCIAL

Crystal Maze for hipsters? Picture House Social is a lynchpin of the now-thriving independent street that is Abbeydale Road. Six years ago, the idea of turning a former snooker hall into whatever it is that PHS is now was seen by many as, well, let's say 'brave'.

There's a bar in there with great cocktails and fine beers, so that's a tick, and some of the best pizza in the city being knocked out of the Italian pizza parlour-come-diner in the back. Don't forget about the games room with ping pong tables and vintage arcade games, and there's even a 24-seat private cinema nestled in there somewhere!

Add in the big outdoor terrace and the rumoured arrival of 'Shuffle Shack' (Deck shuffle board and disco, anyone?) and you have a veritable rabbit warren of distractions to go with your drinks.

Oh, we also hear they've just been granted a 3am license for their bouncing weekend nights, so expect to see PHS become THE final destination after that Abbeydale bar crawl.

Photography by India Hobson.

Picture House Social
383 Abbeydale Road, Nether Edge, Sheffield S7 1FS
@picturehousesoc // @picture_house_social
picture-house-social.co.uk

AVAILABLE ON CITY GRAB

SHEFFIELD TAP

The Sheffield Tap has become one of the most popular pubs in the city since it opened ten years ago. Stop in after work with colleagues, for a pre-match pint on a Saturday or simply to enjoy drinks with friends amidst Edwardian splendour.

Sheffield's restored Grade II-listed railway buildings opened in 2009 as Sheffield Tap, a world beer freehouse. It sits between Sheaf Street and Platform 1b at the train station, housed within the former Edwardian refreshment room and dining rooms. The interior is divided into two areas: the main bar, which was originally a drinking space for 'commoners', and a grand dining room for first class passengers. They're divided by a broad hallway that was originally open to the outside platform, but now forms smaller, more intimate spaces.

The interior of the whole bar creates an atmosphere where everyone feels welcome and comfortable, whether you are with a group of friends out for a big night or simply enjoying a coffee while waiting for a train. The restored former first class dining room features a working microbrewery, The Tapped Brew Co. It usually brews between two and three times a week, and if you like beer then you'll love the aroma of malt and hops wafting through the bar!

The Tap (as it is affectionately referred to) was one of the first bars in Sheffield to showcase beers from around the world and the UK. Thornbridge Brewery has supported the venture from the start, so their locomotive nameplate is mounted in the entrance and you'll always find Jaipur on cask and extremely fresh! The team pride themselves on quality, evidenced by the Cask Mark accreditation and multiple national drinks awards, including several from CAMRA. In 2020, Sheffield Tap was named the CAMRA City Centre Pub of the Year.

The dining room and brewery can be booked out for private events, and The Tap has hosted many wedding receptions, parties and corporate functions with facilities such as a projector, drinks and catering options. The bar itself is so popular that a complaint often heard there is that when people come to Sheffield, they don't go any further than the Sheffield Tap: they plan to go out and visit lots of bars in town, but then they get here and don't leave! As a result, the pub has picked up the nickname the Sheffield Trap. Keep an eye on the time if you've got a train to catch!

Sheffield Tap
Platform 1b, Sheffield
Midland Station, Sheaf
Street, Sheffield S1 2BP
0114 273 7558
@thesheffieldtap
sheffieldtap.com

TWO THIRDS BEER CO.

A bustling craft beer haven in the heart of Abbeydale Road's independent scene, Two Thirds Beer Co. is a dream come true for owners Adam, Ben and Danny.

In late 2018, over a round of cañas on one of Seville's rooftop bars, three beer-loving mates from Sheffield set out to create a neighbourhood craft beer bar that was friendly, relaxed and served only the finest beers you could find.

Fast forward to November 2019 and the doors were open at Two Thirds Beer Co., boasting 16 rotating draught beer lines, a giant craft beer fridge showcasing over 100 different bottles and cans from around the world, as well as an eclectic line-up of spirits, wines, soft drinks and snacks to enjoy in a laidback and unpretentious environment.

They have transformed the former home of a vegan dessert shop into the ultimate modern but cosy hops paradise – with a warm, softly-lit interior, comfy snug booths and a giant glass frontage overlooking the bustling, bohemian stretch of Abbeydale Road. It's the perfect place to grab a drink and watch the Steel City go by.

The bar proudly embraces the smaller than usual two thirds pint measure, encouraging visitors to sample a wider range of ever-changing craft beers and ciders. As mentioned, the concept emerged during a trip owners Ben, Danny and Adam took to Seville, where the caña (a small glass of beer) is the standard serve for drinks. Naturally, good beer is of the highest importance, but the bar has a cracking line-up of gins which are served in their oft-admired retro gin balloons.

Situated right at the centre of Abbeydale Road's popular and vibrant independent quarter, the bar has fast become a favourite of both locals and beer enthusiasts alike. The indoor tables and popular European-style outdoor terrace are regularly packed on weekends and for post-work drinks, so heading down early is a must!

Lockdown also saw Two Thirds launch their online shop, offering the largest selection of takeaway craft beers in Sheffield as well as freshly canned draught beer (all delivered to your door if you live local!) – perfect for gifts, or to treat yourself to the ultimate night in! Keep an eye peeled as there are some exciting expansion plans already in place for next year, starting with the launch of a kitchen in early 2021. We'll raise a glass to that!

AVAILABLE ON CITY GRAB

Two Thirds Beer Co.
434-436 Abbeydale Road,
Sheffield S7 1FQ
@twothirdsbeerco
twothirdsbeer.co

TWO THIRDS

Don't drink Shit beer

BEER CO.

PUBS + BARS

Join us as we continue our crawl of cracking independent pubs and bars in Sheffield. Your round?

Beer Engine // beerenginesheffield.com

A cosy watering hole that prides itself on an ever-changing vast selection of keg and bottled beers. They also have a proper chef, so the food is excellent. Everything is made in-house, with the regular menu consisting of tapas-style small plates that complement the beer.

Tramshed // instagram.com/tramshedbarandkitchen

A cosy bar on Chesterfield Road with an excellent selection of cans, bottles and local beverages on tap. Exposed brickwork, bottles of flowers, candles on tables, vintage lamps and gutter trays filled with plants make up the décor downstairs, while the upstairs space is reserved for exhibitions, cinema screenings and various other cultural happenings. A truly unique spot for a tipple.

Brothers Arms // facebook.com/thebrothersarms

If you find yourself venturing out to Heeley then check out the Brothers Arms. Alongside the usual offerings of booze, food and live grooves, The Brothers Arms also boasts an excellently elevated view over Sheffield to enjoy while you sink down a cold lager, peruse various ales, or chase a cold, sharp and colourful gin and tonic.

Dead Donkey // deaddonkeybar.co.uk

Well known to any frequent visitors to Abbeydale Road's Broadfield pub, brothers Ed and Doug Daly left in 2018 for pastures new, opening up the Dead Donkey just yards down the road. It has quietly built up an excellent reputation in the city for, quite simply, having top class ales and great craft beers on, and their whisky selection is also impressive.

The Cremorne // @TheCremorne

A vibrant little boozer on London Road with a strong community feel, The Cremorne welcomes an eclectic clientele and is celebrated for its live music programme, chilled out atmosphere, rotating guest beer selection and top-notch stonebaked pizzas.

Gardeners Rest // @gardenerscomsoc

This community-owned Neepsend boozer was taken over by its regulars in 2017 and has come on leaps and bounds ever since. Not only are the ales well-priced and local, but the unique beer garden offers a tranquil seat alongside the River Don.

The Red Deer // red-deer-sheffield.co.uk

Easily one of the cosiest boozers in the city centre. This traditional hideout has a decent little beer garden around back for summer sessions and during the winter they'll get the fire going, but all year round you can expect the same standard of quality ales and homely grub.

Firepit Rocks // Firepit.rocks

Rebranding from grilled meats haven FirePit BBQ to FirePit Rocks, this popular late-night establishment is still the place for American cuisine in Sheffield but also channels the classic US dive bar vibe: sports on TV, rock tunes 'til the early hours, quality cocktails and a lively atmosphere.

The Crow Inn // facebook.com/TheCrowInn
Reopened in 2019 by the owners of the popular Rutland Arms, this historic pub went straight on CAMRA's list of notable watering holes, Sheffield's Real Heritage Pubs. The building has a turbulent past, but is now best known for city centre accommodation and a great selection of craft beers.

Shakespeares // shakespeares-sheffield.co.uk
Perfectly placed between Kelham Island and the city centre on the Don Valley Real Ale Trail, Shakespeares boasts a beer garden and plenty of interesting real ales. The cosy pub, formerly a Georgian coaching inn, always provides a friendly welcome, whether you go for the live music or a quiet drink.

Hagglers Corner // facebook.com/hagglers. corner
Reopened in 2020 by The Bhaji Shop gang, this collective of indies has food and drink to enjoy undercover in the courtyard day and night. Guitar Shack, a music shop selling new and used instruments, and Running With Scissors, who run a variety of crafting courses, are two of the resident businesses at Hagglers. The unique venue is also available to hire for birthday parties, weddings, meetings and other events.

The Grapes
Famed as being the place where the Arctic Monkeys played their first ever gig, there's far more to this historic Irish boozer than that. It's a charming no-nonsense pub, wonderfully cosy on chilly evenings, and hosts regular traditional Irish music sessions and live acoustic on weekends. They don't make 'em like this anymore.

The Dog & Partridge // @thedogsheffield
You're always guaranteed a warm welcome at The Dog, a proud Irish pub with a cracking selection of craft beer, ales and spirits to peruse. Naturally, it serves one of the best pints of Guinness in the city and boasts one of the most inviting little snugs you'll come across, fittingly equipped with a little service hatch to the bar to keep things easy.

Molly Malones // molly-malones.co.uk
An Irish-themed party tavern popular with the student crowd, Molly's provides plenty of craic throughout the evening with regular live music nights, drinks offers and DJ sets. It's a lively spot during the day too, with plenty of live sport and tasty bar food deals to keep you going. Sláinte!

The Dorothy Pax // dorothypax.com
A picturesque gem situated in the Sheffield canal basin, this quirky spot has established itself as a popular summertime hangout with its extended beer garden by the water. It's the perfect spot for escaping the hectic city centre confines, grabbing a drink with friends and watching the boats go by.

The Rutland Arms // rutlandarmssheffield.co.uk
A traditional boozer known for fantastic real ale offerings and a delightful suntrap beer garden. Inside it's comfy and traditional with a jukebox on offer – but please take heed of the forbidden music rules listed on the chalkboard next to it. It offers an enticing menu of homely pub food with changing daily specials, solid vegan offerings and their famous 'Rutty Butty'.

CAFÉS

1554 COFFEE AND GIFT SHOP

Situated in the heart of Sheffield Cathedral, 1554 Coffee and Gift Shop is a beautiful haven celebrating what the city has to offer. Here local suppliers are celebrated, coffee unites the community and regulars have been coming back for years.

The Cathedral has been a key part of Sheffield for over 100 years, and it is this sense of community that is really encompassed in 1554.

"It's more than just a coffee shop," says manager Ruth. "Regulars come in to see a friendly face and for a fun day out. We offer a peaceful place for people to escape from the busy city centre and play an important role in the working life of the Cathedral."

The rich religious history of the Cathedral with its grand architecture fused with 1554's contemporary gifts and independent produce creates an exciting mix. Ruth and her team really wanted to cherish what makes Sheffield so special, building relationships with local independent businesses and engaging with customers old and new. Sheffield coffee favourite Heavenly Coffee Co has given them their own barista blend for making fantastic coffee, dairy is supplied by Our Cow Molly and the whole counter is completely sourced from areas around the city. There are also local gifts sold aplenty, with a full range of Sheffield icon Henderson's Relish as well as several flavours of luxuriously indulgent Sheffield Honey.

The café, which has a spacious interior with dazzling stained glass windows, is one that is certainly not to be missed. The staff work really hard to ensure that they have a variety of fresh and hearty food every day, which includes veggie, vegan and gluten-free, stocking up with wonderful goodies like the always popular meat and potato pie, a gorgeous deli counter and even some Bakewell Bakery originals for if you fancy a sweet treat.

1554 works with the Cathedral, bringing in that extra customer who perhaps wouldn't normally visit. It is always busy with a real mix of people; its welcoming feel and unpretentious ambience is testament to Ruth and the team's effort to make it a place where the whole community can feel at home. What makes it truly amazing is that all proceeds go back to the working life of the Cathedral, which really helps to integrate the café and gift shop into Sheffield life.

With 1554 always on the hunt for new independent produce to work with and sell, it is set to remain an important part of Sheffield Cathedral and the city for many more years to come.

1554 Coffee
and Gift Shop
Sheffield Cathedral,
Church Street,
Sheffield S1 1HA
0114 2636074
sheffieldcathedral.org

ALBIES

Albies Coffee is an inviting space ready to welcome you in. Brother and sister duo Robyn and Fraser opened this stylish coffee house aged just 23 and 24, and a stop for their quality selection of coffee has become an everyday ritual for many.

With Albie being the name of their grandfather, the coffee shop pays a touching tribute. "He was an amazing, welcoming and totally fun-loving person," says Robyn, a personality which is reciprocated in this intimate haven. The siblings created Albies with the belief that speciality coffee should be accessible for all and Sheffield is the ideal location, a smaller city with a bigger space to flourish. Their goal is to create a familiar spot with friendly faces that brings a sense of community to the changing face of Castlegate.

The house espresso is roasted in Attercliffe by Cuppers Choice. Big bodied, bright and carrying well through milk, this blend hits just the spot, be it in your morning brew or lazier afternoon fix (usually sipped alongside something laced in sugar – almond croissants are a favourite!). Things get a little jazzier on the guest filter; refills are a quid and it's your opportunity to try out some of the finer things from speciality roasters all over the UK. 'Reyt good coffee for reyt good people' is the motto here, but the loaded bagels and grilled cheese sandwiches are popular too if you fancy it!

Retail is a major part of the business, with a fantastic selection of coffee beans and equipment tailored perfectly to your preferences. Stuck on how to brew? Here's a quick and easy guide!

Equipment

Scales
Timer
Server
Pouring Kettle
Medium coarse ground coffee
Hario 02 V60 and 02 filter papers

Ingredients

20g coffee
310ml hot water

Method

Position the V60 on top of the server. Open the filter paper up and place inside the V60, rinse with hot water to eliminate the papery taste, then empty the server.

Replace the server underneath V60 and add the coffee, then tap to level the coffee bed. Reset the scale to zero, start the timer and pour 50-65g hot water over the coffee. Next, give the V60 a slow whirl, making sure all the grounds become wet. This is called the bloom.

After 35-45 seconds pour over the rest of the hot water slowly in a clockwise motion. Now leave until the last bit of water has drained from the top of the coffee bed, remove the V60 from your server and enjoy!

Albies Coffee Ltd
22 Snig Hill,
Sheffield,
S3 8NB
info@albiescoffee.co.uk
@albiessheffield
albiescoffee.co.uk

BAKED & CAKED

Andy and Wendy Dillon adapted quickly to the UK's lockdown in March 2020, fearing they would lose enough customers of their wholesale bakery business to potentially shut their growing enterprise down. Having found a great location on Chesterfield Road, the couple opened a brand new cake shop, Baked & Caked, on the 1st August in what they admitted was a "scary and risky move" that has happily proved a great success with the locals.

What really makes the little shop stand out are the unique vegan products that Wendy creates. A pastry chef by trade, she began a brownie business that branched out amidst a crowded market into Scoffingtons. Wendy dreamt up these irresistible sweet treats when Lola, her daughter, asked whether you could get Lamingtons without the coconut; Scoffingtons are a square of light sponge cake, dipped in chocolate ganache, coated in biscuit crumb and topped with frosting. Following some experimentation with flavours and techniques, a vegan version joined the product lines of Hash Brownies, and soon found itself a loyal following.

That was when the coronavirus hit, and the orders ground to a halt. Wendy and Andy have made the most of this new chapter with Baked & Caked though, coming up with new ideas to expand their range from just two products to dozens. "The shop has allowed us to express creativity again," explains Andy. "The ability to diversify is important for small businesses like ours, and we want to continue being innovative while catering for our customers here in Meersbrook and Yorkshire."

A great example of their outside-the-box thinking is the #bronut, another of Wendy's inventions, which is a baked or fried doughnut made with brioche dough, that also happens to be vegan. Needless to say, it's one of the bakery's most popular products, alongside vegan Danish pastries, croissants and savoury treats. Although they supplied baked goods to many local venues, participated in the Sheffield Food Festival, and provided dessert for one of Eat Sheffield's awards events, Andy and Wendy weren't known directly to their fans as a wholesale business. Now, they enjoy the regular contact with customers in the shop, which has saved eight years of hard work that led up to it, and feel thankful for where they are right now.

Baked & Caked
55 Chesterfield Road,
Meersbrook,
Sheffield S8 0RL
0114 327 2618
bakedandcaked.co.uk

BAKED & CAKED FAVES

Andy and Wendy Dillon introduce you to some of their favourite creations from Baked & Caked.

The Banoffington

One of our very favourite creations from recent years is known as a Banoffington. It's a delicious cube of banana and caramel cake fully covered in ganache, coated with a ginger biscuit crumb and topped with fudge pieces and chocolate curls. It proved to be so good we decided to trademark the name. This was the first dipped-style cake we sold, and paved the way towards Scoffingtons. We then expanded on this concept to produce other firm favourites that currently include pistachio and cherry, Malteaser, and passion fruit with chilli chocolate and coconut. Watch this space!

Scoffingtons

After the creation of our popular and unique dipped cakes, Wendy wanted to create something that was enjoyed by both vegan and non-vegan customers. Trials, errors and lots of tasting led us to the vegan chocolate cake we turned into the Scoffingtons. We launched the range at Sheffield Food Festival and they became an instant hit! We then added them to our wholesale list and Scoffingtons are now served in numerous coffee shops, restaurants, students' unions and even a cinema. With our ever expanding flavour choices there is something to suit everyone's taste buds.

Bronuts

For a few years our wholesale business was pretty much centred around the production of Brownies and Scoffingtons. Then along came our little den of delectable delights, so more creativity was needed. We had previously become a victim of our own success with our specially devised Bronuts. They didn't really work as a wholesale product so we decided to bring them back and re-invent them as a vegan version that we could sell in the shop at weekends. We now have flavours that include sour cherry and almond, pumpkin spice, salted toffee and the original cinnamon.

Croissants and Danish Pastries

Many moons ago, Wendy trained with the Roux brothers and spent some time perfecting croissants. After requests from customers at Baked & Caked, she decided it was time to re-flour the rolling pin and create a vegan croissant dough and a vegan puff pastry that were as delicious as anything you'd find in a French patisserie. We stepped up to the challenge and were able to produce something that is thoroughly enjoyed by our customers. Our offerings at the shop now include croissants, Danish pastries, pain au chocolat, pain au raisin and a selection of savoury vegan and vegetarian pastries.

Baked & Caked
55 Chesterfield Road, Meersbrook, Sheffield S8 0RL
0114 327 2618
bakedandcaked.co.uk

BIRDHOUSE TEA CO.

Tea purveyors and artisan blenders Birdhouse Tea Co. have been producing delicious Sheffield-inspired tea since opening in 2013.

Birdhouse Tea Co. are Sheffield's favourite tea blenders, with many of their teas blended as love letters to our fine city.

They won a gold star in the Great Taste Awards for their breakfast blend, Full Monty, which they serve alongside hundreds of other teas, cocktails and innovative drinks at their tea bar and kitchen on Sidney Street in the city centre of Sheffield. Housed in a renovated brick-built factory, the tea bar showcases a multitude of ways to enjoy a great cuppa with brunch dishes, wood-fired pizza and a counter of delicious baked goods.

Birdhouse's famous tea lattes are a must-try, especially their signature 'Sheffield Fog'. Aromatic earl grey, sweet vanilla and steamed milk makes for the most comforting cup and is so easy to create at home.

SHEFFIELD FOG

Ingredients
10g Birdhouse Earl Grey
350ml boiling water
1 vanilla pod
50g sugar
250ml milk or dairy-free alternative

Method

Infuse the Birdhouse Earl Grey in 250ml of boiling water and steep for 5 minutes. Once brewed, strain the leaves to create a strong concentrate to form the base of your tea latte.

Put the remaining 100ml of boiling water into a pan with the sugar and the whole vanilla pod, then simmer gently for 5 minutes. Remove the vanilla pod, and decant your syrup into a heatproof jar.

Add the milk to a pan and heat gently before whisking to create frothy milk. Top tip: add the heated milk to a cafetière pot and begin to plunge for 10-20 seconds.

Add 100ml of tea concentrate to your favourite mug along with 50ml of the homemade vanilla syrup.

Top with hot steamed milk and finish with a sprinkle of cornflower petals for garnish.

Your concentrate and syrup will store in the fridge for two days.

**Birdhouse Tea Co.
Sidney Street,
Sheffield S1 4RG**

@birdhouseteabarandkitchen
birdhouseteacompany.com

BLUE MOON CAFÉ

Established by Bill Clarke and Nick Dunhill, Blue Moon Café began life in 1995 on Norfolk Row, inspired by a shared love of veggie and vegan food. During the planning stages, the name was used as a working title, influenced by a catering stall at Glastonbury Festival, and as the opening approached no better name came to mind and Blue Moon was the winner!

The café moved to its current location on St James Street in 2001. Situated near Sheffield Cathedral, it truly is the most beautiful spot. A trip there today is stepping into history; the building dates back to 1865 when it was built as an auction hall for the estate agent Eadon Lockwood and Riddle. The current décor is like a 19th century painting, with an angelic skylight ceiling providing a source of illumination, creating a heavenly light-filled glow.

It's important to Kitchen Manager Rosa that they provide something different whilst also paying homage to classic dishes. To this end, the café draws on a range of inspirations: from the traditionally British homity pie to their imam bayildi, which is a Turkish roast aubergine and tomato dish and a popular favourite according to Rosa: "We couldn't take it off the menu without getting a lot of complaints!" Excitingly, they change up the salad menu weekly, taking inspiration from here, there and everywhere. Above all, they concentrate on keeping the food fresh whilst exhibiting a vibrant explosion of colours on the plate.

As well as serving delicious food from around the world, they also pride themselves on sourcing their produce as locally as possible, collaborating with Girls Who Grind Coffee, an ethical and empowering initiative to support female coffee growers.

Over the years they have accumulated a number of awards, including the 'Best Place for Vegan/Vegetarian Food' in the 2018 Social Sheffield Awards. They have also carried out some amazing charity work, having raised almost £600 for ASSIST's Sponsor a Room campaign. ASSIST is a local charity supporting refugees in Sheffield, and in recent years Blue Moon partnered with them by offering free meals on Monday evenings.

They know first-hand that small independent businesses need our ongoing support due to the challenges of the pandemic, as they recently fundraised £5000 for unexpected repairs. After being overwhelmed by the generosity of their customers, they managed to raise the full amount in just 72 hours! Sheffield as a community has kept them afloat, and they could not be prouder of the city they live in.

Blue Moon Café
2 St James Street,
Sheffield, S1 2EW
0114 276 3443
bluemooncafe@hotmail.
co.uk
Instagram:
@bluemoonsheffield
Facebook:
@bluemooncafesheffield

THE GRIND

The Grind recently celebrated its ten year anniversary thanks to the vision and dedication of owners Howard and Amanda, as well as their hard-working team.

Back in 2010, the now prime location was almost a brownfield site, set amongst the former factories of Kelham Island, so opening an artisan coffee shop there was a brave move. However, as Howard says, "if you've got a good product, people will come and find you" which is exactly what's happened at this longstanding independent. Though Kelham is now a hugely popular place to live, work and socialise, The Grind is still a destination eatery that's part daytime restaurant, part cosy coffee shop. The early days saw regular visits from the Arctic Monkeys, and today it's equally popular with local residents and nearby businesses for coffee breaks and meetings.

Visitors are presented with a counter full of healthy, homemade food that ranges from sandwiches to stews alongside the signature seasonal salads. There's also a tempting display of indulgent cakes and sweet treats to enjoy with a hot drink, or even a glass of wine. Croissants are the only item bought in; everything else is made on site by the chefs. The café has served vegan and gluten-free food since day one, using fresh vegetables, fish and meat to create delicious options for a range of tastes and diets.

"A lot of the creativity in the food and our offering at The Grind comes from Amanda," says Howard. "We're the café's biggest critics so from that point of view there's always something to improve, which means we've evolved over the years, although our loyal customer base keep coming back for old favourites like the giant sausage rolls!"

They know that small independent businesses need that kind of ongoing support to be successful, so despite the challenges 2020 has presented, the owners are confident that continuing to do the right thing will keep The Grind afloat. They also offer outside catering for events such as weddings, which they've done lots of recently. To adapt in these difficult times, Howard and Amanda are also considering a takeaway service at some point in the future. For now though, the well-loved café continues to serve customers safely throughout the day, from full English breakfasts to the last slice of cake, and remains a proudly independent Sheffield hotspot.

The Grind
Cornwall Works, 3 Green
Lane, Kelham Island,
Sheffield S3 8SJ
0114 272 3929
grindcafe.co.uk

THE GRIND'S LAMB TAGINE

This is a great dish for when you have friends coming over, and can be made a day in advance. Serve it on a large platter in the middle of the table topped with natural yoghurt, pomegranate seeds and chopped coriander for a colourful, visual feast that everyone can dig into.

Preparation time: 30 minutes | Cooking time: 2 hours | Serves 4

Ingredients

1.5kg diced lamb
2 tbsp olive oil
3 large white onions, chopped
20g garlic, finely chopped
1 cinnamon stick
Pinch of chilli flakes
50g ground cumin
40g ground coriander
20g fresh ginger, peeled and finely chopped
250ml fresh orange juice
800g good quality passata
325ml chicken stock
300g cooked chickpeas, drained
100g whole dried apricots
80g juicy golden sultanas
80g fresh coriander, chopped
Light brown sugar, to taste
Salt and black pepper

Method

Season the lamb with salt and pepper, then brown in batches for 4 to 5 minutes in a hot pan with a little oil. Transfer the sealed meat to a bowl and set aside.

Put the chopped onions into the same pan you browned the lamb in, add seasoning and fry over a medium heat until golden which should take about 5 minutes.

Now add the chopped garlic, all the spices and the fresh ginger to the onions. Stir for 1 minute, making sure nothing catches and burns. Pour in the orange juice and passata, then stir in the lamb and bring up to the boil.

Add the chicken stock and bring back to the boil, then reduce to a low heat, cover and simmer until the lamb is really tender. This takes around 2 hours.

Once the lamb is ready, stir in the cooked chickpeas, apricots, sultanas and chopped coriander. Season the tagine with sugar, salt and pepper to taste.

To serve

Transfer your tagine into a large presentation dish, then top with natural yoghurt, pomegranate seeds and chopped coriander. Try serving it with couscous, toasted pitta or flatbreads to dip into the tagine and mop up the gorgeous sauce.

The Grind
Cornwall Works, 3 Green Lane, Kelham Island, Sheffield S3 8SJ
0114 272 3929
grindcafe.co.uk

JAMESON'S PLOUGHMANS RAREBIT

Jameson's Tearoom & Kitchens specialise in afternoon teas, homemade cakes, breakfast and lunches. All the food on the extensive menu is freshly prepared and can be enjoyed with a range of loose leaf teas or your favourite tipple amidst the elegant yet contemporary décor, or at home in a Jameson's hamper.

Preparation time: 10 minutes | Cooking time: 10 minutes | Serves 2

This recipe is a fusion of their customers' most popular dishes: the infamous ploughman's lunch, a plate filled with locally sourced delicacies, and the rarebit which is packed full of flavour and has the ultimate comfort factor.

Ingredients

4 slices of thick cut bloomer bread (white or granary)
2 large eggs
190g red cheddar cheese, grated
150g hand-carved ham, shredded
80g mature cheddar cheese, grated
80g Branston pickle
60g blue Stilton, crumbled

Method

First, lightly toast the sliced bread. Crack the eggs into a bowl, beat lightly with a fork, then add the remaining ingredients. Mix everything together until well combined.

Top the toasted bread with the cheesy mixture, covering one side of each slice. Place the rarebit under a grill on medium heat until the topping starts to melt. At this point, turn up the temperature for the grill to cook the rarebit until glazed, bubbly and golden.

Serve your rarebit with some pork pie, pickles and a crisp green salad for the best fusion ploughman's lunch. Enjoy!

Jameson's Tearoom
& Kitchens
334-336 Abbeydale Road,
Sheffield, S7 1SN
0114 255 1159

enquire@
jamesonstearooms.co.uk
@jamesonstearooms

LOTTE ON THE EDGE

Nether Edge's eclectic café Lotte On The Edge is inspired by owner Charlotte Carey's trips to Isla Mujeres in Mexico, bringing back with her an array of colourful décor, unpretentious food and a vibrant atmosphere in a cosy little spot in the friendly Sheffield suburb.

Reopening and rebranding as Lotte on the Edge in 2017, the popular café fell into the hands of owner Charlotte Carey by chance three years ago. By fate, Lotte On The Edge was born after a split with a former business partner, after which she began to inject her bubbly personality into the venue.

"I transformed the interior of the café when I bought it," Charlotte tells us. "I wanted to give it a beach bar vibe so that's what I keep calling it! An urban beach café. Inside there's a lot of wood, I painted the ceiling black, I have these Mexican pom poms dotted around from my holidays there, cacti, hanging plants, it's all very organic. It's somewhere I'd like to hang out."

It's fair to say that Charlotte's colourful character is etched into the décor of the place, and it's perhaps this approachability and affability which has seen this café become a popular spot among the Nether Edger community and beyond.

"When I bought this, a lot of people said there'd be no footfall and it'd be a bad move," Charlotte adds. "I could see the advantage of having such a lovely outside space – we're south facing so we have the sun in the morning right through to 8pm. We have a lot of regulars too. We can seat about 16 inside and people would say to me that they'd drive past and see the windows steamed up every time and wonder what was inside!"

Her trips to Mexico, more specifically Isla Mujeres near Cancú§n, are clearly inspirational. "I just love the people, they are so friendly. The colours are amazing; it's such a bright, happy place," she says. The café's approach to non-pretentious food and serving up coffee roasted by Dark Woods Coffee from Huddersfield, Lotte On The Edge is an inspired choice, too. Who'd have thought it? An urban beach café in Sheffield, South Yorkshire!

Lotte On The Edge
14 Union Road,
Sheffield, S11 9EF
0114 258 0011
lotteontheedge.com

CAFÉS // The Little Book of Sheffield

VITTLES

Nestled in the bustling area of Broomhill, Vittles is a quaint spot serving up some of the best breakfasts in the city.

Run by husband and wife Mick and Paula, the duo were looking for a lifestyle change, seizing the opportunity when they could. It turned out to be more than they could've ever dreamed of, as this popular business is now the oldest surviving independent café in Sheffield, becoming a very important part of the coffee and brunch culture in the city.

For many, the day begins at Vittles. They serve locally roasted coffee and a great choice of breakfast including full English, which can come veggie or vegan, eggs Benedict, mixed grill and an indulgent stack of syrup-soaked American pancakes. The afternoons are equally as tasty, with a range of sandwiches including the mouth-watering royal CBLT and the vegan Beyond Burger, and the majority of the menu can be adapted to be gluten-free. All the food is freshly prepared each day, which also means that dishes can be altered to suit various requirements that a customer may have. At a great price, this homely, quality menu is perfect for warming the soul on a rainy day.

Every part of this comfortable café is fun yet traditional; the interior is cosy and friendly, with personable, consistently good service, as well as plenty of pictures of Sheffield on the walls, truly showcasing a strong Yorkshire sentiment. Vittles marries indulgent food with warm surroundings and an old-English, comfortable set-up, making you feel right at home.

They pride themselves on being local, sourcing their meat products from the award-winning Moss Valley Farm, as well as free-range eggs and dairy from Town End Farm. Their chosen coffee roasters are Sheffield's Heavenly Coffee Company, and they also purchase from Crawshaws Butchers and local greengrocers Fruit a Peel. Whatever the menu reads, the food is undoubtedly almost completely found in Sheffield, readily embracing the produce that the city has to offer.

Over the years they have served thousands of students, locals and some celebrities, including musical icons Coldplay and the Arctic Monkeys. They have always ensured the café is open to anyone; families and visitors of all ages are among their many regular customers for whom the place is a part of their identity. It's hard to imagine Broomhill without Vittles inviting in passers-by; it is an important corner of Sheffield, and Mick and Paula are hopeful that locals will continue to support them for many more years to come.

AVAILABLE ON CITY GRAB

Vittles Café
501A Glossop Road,
Sheffield S10 2QE
0114 268 2857
vittlesofsheffield.com

WHALETOWN'S VEGAN MOCHA PANCAKES

The Whaletown Coffee Company is an award-winning speciality coffee shop in Crookes, serving Cuppers Choice Coffee Roasters on house and guesting different European Roasters every month. For a small place it has made a big impact nationally for its consistency, customer service, and dedication to sustainability and coffee industry innovation.

Preparation time: 10 minutes | Cooking time: 10 minutes | Serves 2-4

Owner Jordan O'Shea has shared a delicious recipe that combines your morning coffee with an indulgent yet plant-based breakfast. What's not to love?

For the pancakes

125g self-raising flour (can be gluten-free)

1 tsp baking powder

Pinch of sea salt

150ml Oatly Chocolate Oat Drink

½ tsp vanilla extract

1 double espresso (40ml)

Coconut oil, for frying

Mixed fruits, to serve

For the mocha syrup

1 heaped tbsp vegan chocolate powder

1 double espresso

Who doesn't love a pancake? They're perfect as breakfast or dessert, and the only way to make these even better is, of course, by adding coffee! For this, I am using a washed Nicaragua Jinotega double espresso from Sheffield's own Cuppers Choice Coffee Roasters. I understand not everyone has access to an espresso machine in their home, so I suggest either bringing home a double espresso from your favourite local, or if you have a Nespresso pod machine, get the pods from Colonna & Small's or April Coffee Roasters, for example.

For the pancakes

Put the flour, baking powder, and sea salt into a large bowl and thoroughly mix them together. Add the chocolate oat drink, vanilla extract and double espresso, and whisk them together until the batter is smooth and looks so good you want to lick it off your whisk.

Heat a frying pan and add a teaspoon of coconut oil. Spread the oil around the pan, then add about 2 tablespoons of the pancake batter into the centre of the pan and spread with the back of a spoon in a circular motion. Cook the pancake until bubbles appear on the surface, then flip to the other side and cook for a further minute, allowing the pancake to rise and become fluffy. Place the pancake on a baking tray in the oven on a low heat to keep warm while you make the rest.

For the mocha syrup

Put the vegan chocolate powder in a small bowl or mug, add the double espresso, and mix together with a fork until the powder has dissolved and the mixture resembles a thick, dark sauce.

To serve

Stack your pancakes on a plate, pour the syrup all over them, and add any fresh fruit you desire. Easy. Tasty. Caffeine dream.

Whaletown Coffee Co.
227 Crookes,
Sheffield, S10 1TE
www.whaletowncoffee.com
whaletowncoffeeco@gmail.com
Follow us on social media
@whaletowncoffeeco

CAFÉS

Fancy a cuppa? Here are a few more of your favourite cafe spots in the Steel City.

Blend Kitchen // www.blendcookeatshare.com
Blend Kitchen is a social enterprise run by a chef who decided to put his unique combination of skills to good use. This café with a conscience creates food-led initiatives to vulnerable or disadvantaged people, alongside offering an eclectic menu to eat in or take away that's inspired by Sheffield's cultural melting pot.

Steamyard // steamyard.co.uk
Nestled in a picturesque courtyard off Division Street, this popular café is a charming spot serving up some of the best coffee and doughnuts you'll find up north. It's that good people love to shout about it, and in 2019 it became the most instagrammed independent coffee shop in the UK.

Gaard // facebook.com/GaardCoffee
Gaard is a cosy coffee shop with tons of hearty breakfast options, as well as vegan sourdough croissants, smoothies and sweet treats.

Whether you're after a light bite or a slap up breakfast, Gaard has grown into one of the finest cafés in the city – even branching out into the city centre in 2020.

Marmadukes // marmadukes.co
Small but mighty, Marmadukes offers the best of British food and drink with an exciting range of options from breakfast through to lunch, including a full English breakfast for under a tenner with vegetarian options available too. The perfect place to go for a hearty Sunday brekkie after a hectic weekend. It's worth visiting their huge new venue in the city centre as part of the Heart of the City development.

South Street Kitchen // southstreetkitchen.org
Situated in Park Hill flats just above the train station, this independent coffee space with a focus on community and Middle Eastern food is the very definition of a hidden gem. Knock back a Dark Woods coffee, craft beer or a wine, and for food sample the falafel and flatbreads.

Ambulo // weareambulo.com
A collaborative effort from co-founder of the Rockingham Group (the team behind Public, Picture House Social and Gatsby) James O'Hara and Arctic Monkeys drummer Matt Helders, the first Ambulo all-day café opened in the Millennium Gallery in 2019, followed by a second venue at the Weston Park Museum shortly after. The bosses sum it up nicely: "It's a place for a slap-up dinner, a coffee and an Aperol Spritz."

Tamper // tampercoffee.co.uk

A strong café scene means brunch spots are aplenty around here, but Arundel Street's Tamper Coffee is something of a Steel City Mecca for early munching – that good, in fact, it's been lauded as one of the best breakfast spots in the country by the Guardian and Waitrose Good Food Magazine. There's also a picturesque courtyard for some al fresco action on sunny days.

Forge Bakehouse // forgebakehouse.co.uk

This bakery has earnt itself the title of 'artisan' through and through; the bakers, chefs and baristas make everything from scratch, ready for the counter and café seven days a week. Pick up a pastry, try your hand at home baking with their pantry supplies, or grab a loaf to enjoy some of the best bread in the city.

Island // facebook.com/IslandKelham

This light and airy café is right next door to The Millowners Arms in Kelham's museum quarter, and is the perfect spot for breakfast, brunch and lunch with a menu of contemporary takes on firm favourites. Pop in for a hot drink and a fry up or grab a sandwich to enjoy on the go.

Cole's Corner // facebook.com/ColesCornerSheffield

Inspired by the laidback social vibes of small café-come-record shops in Amsterdam, the recently opened Cole's Corner provides a cosy haven for vinyl-lovers and specialises in reggae, drum 'n' bass, jungle, afrobeat, and world music, plus local Sheffield-made music of any genre. Using locally sourced produce, here you can enjoy seasonal food such as homely organic soups, paninis, a range of hot and cold drinks, and an evening beer or two courtesy of Abbeydale Brewery.

MAKERS

4EYES' CHOCOLATE & HAZELNUT BABKA

Preparation time: 30 minutes, plus proving | Cooking time: approx. 25 minutes | Serves 12

This recipe is a firm favourite at 4eyes HQ after the team were asked to make it by one of their customers!

4eyes was brought to life with a clear concept: supply premium quality cakes, patisserie and viennoiserie to local businesses. 4eyes now supplies to a wide array of businesses all over Yorkshire and Derbyshire. The small, close knit team consists of Matthew, Stuart, Theo, Jamie, Libby and Matt. They've always tried to focus on using the best quality ingredients and enjoy evolving their product lists to complement the seasons, which have expanded to include very popular vegan, gluten-free and savoury items.

4eyes
Unit 3D, Thornhill Industrial Estate, Hope Street, Rotherham, S60 1LH
07972914037
@4eyespatisserie

For the dough
500g plain flour
60g caster sugar
5g salt
25g dried yeast
125g butter
2 medium eggs
125ml milk

For the filling
60g butter
90g caster sugar
50g 70% dark chocolate
25g cocoa powder
5g ground cinnamon
50g hazelnuts, toasted and lightly crushed

For the syrup
50g caster sugar
50g glucose

For the dough
Put everything, except the eggs and milk, into a stand mixer with a dough hook attachment. Mix for 2 minutes at medium speed, then add the milk and eggs and let it combine for 5 minutes. Leave the dough in the bowl and make the filling.

For the filling
Melt the butter and put all the other ingredients, except the hazelnuts, into a bowl. Stir the hot butter into the bowl, mix to a paste and then set aside at room temperature.

Line a 30cm loaf tin with baking paper and roll out the dough into a rectangle 2cm wider than the tin. Spread the chocolate filling over the dough and sprinkle over the hazelnuts. Roll up the dough, starting from the top and rolling towards yourself. Make sure the roll is tight as it tends to separate.

Now cut down the centre of the roll lengthways. Lay one of the pieces on top of the other with the chocolate layers facing up. Twist the pieces together starting from the middle; you should get three turns at each end. Gently scrunch the twist from each end to make the babka plumper and fit the tin.

Transfer the babka into the lined tin and press down gently. Cover and leave to prove somewhere warm until doubled in size. Bake the proved babka in a preheated fan oven for 16 minutes at 190°c and then turn the temperature down to 170°c for another 8 minutes.

For the syrup
While it bakes, put the sugar and glucose in a small pan with 50ml of water and heat until the sugars have dissolved. Before taking the babka out of the tin, douse it generously with the syrup and then leave to cool. Slice and serve the babka on its own or with honey, cream or more chocolate. Enjoy! Try swapping out the chocolate and replace it with apple and raisin, blueberry and pistachio or any other favourite flavours too.

CITY GRAB

Bringing together an exciting selection of independent eateries and takeaways, the aim of CityGrab is to provide a fairer service and keep money firmly within the local economy.

With the aim of supporting our local independents and putting money back into the local economy, City Taxis launched their own takeaway delivery app in early 2020. Not only was this a huge success, bringing some of the city's incredible food and drink spots to the homes of Sheffielders, the delivery service launched at a critical time for the hospitality industry with lockdown restrictions in place.

It's more efficient than its rivals as City have 2,000 drivers on the road, completing 150,000 journeys every week. This allows them to deliver further and faster than their competitors. Going hand-in-hand with the local focus, CityGrab charges fairer commission rates to businesses on the app. These are 50% less when compared to typical discounts offered by global food delivery giants… plus the taxi driver delivering the food receives all the delivery fare too.

There are over 300 top-notch eateries on the app, such as Beres (whose famous pork sandwiches fly out of the door), Kommune (where you can order from multiple outlets all at once), Oisoi, Our Cow Molly, Proove Pizza, The Broadfield, Street Food Chef and Ashoka, as well as loads more across the city.

It's all about supporting your local businesses, keeping your city's economy strong, and providing fresh choice from your favourite Sheffield food vendors and restaurants.

But food was just the start of it. Towards the end of 2020, CityGrab expanded their online marketplace to retail, hoping to support indies during the Christmas rush, usually dominated by the likes of Amazon and other huge conglomerates, with the likes of Henderson's Relish selling their branded merch on the app.

CityGrab is available on the App Store and Google Play store. Download the app, browse the menus on offer, pop in your address and your food will be on its way.

If you are a restaurant interested in joining email phil.turner@ citygrab.co.uk

EXPOSED MAGAZINE

For the best part of two decades, Exposed has faithfully served as Sheffield's definitive entertainment, lifestyle and culture magazine.

Established in 2003, the free publication provides a monthly guide to Steel City culture, clubbing, food and drink, music, and anything else worth shouting about in 10,000 copies distributed around the city's bars, cafés, shops and local businesses.

"We're passionate about the city and want to promote all the hardworking businesses and individuals doing their thing here," says Exposed editor Joseph Food. "Whether it's showcasing local musicians and artists or highlighting new places to eat and drink, it's our job to cover all of that and make sure people here know what a cracking place this is to live."

Each year the magazine hosts the Exposed Awards, a big annual do bigging up the best of Sheffield. Readers vote for their favourite businesses in the city across 20+ categories and on the night an awards ceremony is held to announce the winners, usually interspersed with live music and followed by one or two raucous afterparties.

The magazine is also known for its long-running Exposed: In Session series which showcases Sheffield's ever-evolving music scene, filming live performances in a variety of interesting locations ranging from a cathedral to an old steelworks. "We're spoiled when it comes to music and art in this city," says Joseph. "The sessions are a way of shining a light on that, and we've had some fantastic acts over the years including Steve 'Papa' Edwards, Drenge and Slow Club – to more recent sessions with the likes of Jackie Moonbather, Otis Mensah, Blackwaters and LIO. They're all on Facebook and YouTube and definitely worth trawling through."

Naturally, the publication works closely with local events, and for a number of years now has compiled an annual newspaper celebrating Tramlines Festival and a booklet promoting the Tramlines Fringe. It has also worked on guides for Sheffield Food Festival, Sheffield Beer Week and Sensoria, not to mention compiling special issues for Sheffield Doc/Fest and No Bounds Festival.

Moving forward, Joseph says the publication is looking to continue with its mission of promoting independent businesses in the city along with the talent propping up its music and arts scene. "It's been a tough year for many businesses, but we're hoping for a more positive 2021 where the city can get safely back on its two feet. The people in this city are incredible when it comes to supporting local independents, and we're going to continue letting them know exactly how they can do so."

Exposed Magazine
0114 275 7709
@ExposedMagSheff
exposedmagazine.co.uk

FRAZER'S COFFEE ROASTERS

Using their own roaster made from the finest Sheffield steel, Frazer's Coffee source beans from around the world and create exciting blends distributed to businesses across South Yorkshire.

Frazer Habershon's passion for coffee started at home. When it came to brewing up, his mum would always ensure there were good quality beans around, but it would take a few years for the Sheffield lad to go from avid coffee drinker to building one of the city's best-known independent roasters.

Frazer worked at a number of pubs and cafés including Caffe Latte and Tamper Sellers Wheel in Sheffield – the latter being particularly instrumental in igniting a passion for the industry that saw him start experimenting at home using a small roaster purchased online.

Roasting initially for himself, Frazer later began passing out samples to neighbours, who were impressed and began placing orders. Word quickly got around and he was approached by a trader in Meadowhall to see if he was interested in roasting for their shop. It was a huge jump, which provided something of a baptism of fire for Frazer's Coffee, the first major step in a pretty remarkable journey for the company.

"At that point I decided to go and open premises in Attercliffe," Frazer tells us. "My mum was instrumental in me taking that step; she persuaded me to open the company in my name. The initial confidence and belief instilled in me was through her being such a foodie, and since then she's been a huge part of it all – behind the stall with me at events, always at the roastery, and just generally being a great, supportive mum."

After researching the market and setting up the company, Frazer went from roasting a couple of kilos of coffee a week to around 40 or 50 kilos. So, in true Yorkshire DIY style, Frazer got his hands dirty and built a bigger coffee roaster out of an old barbecue. It was in action at the first ever Peddler Market in 2014 and facilitated the company's development into a fully-fledged wholesale business.

The growth continued, seeing the company twice move to larger premises. Whilst based at their Carbrook location, a need to upgrade roasters returned again. Holding true to the company's strong 'made in Sheffield' ethos, Frazer purchased a 12 kilo roasting drum – all the company could afford at the time – and set about making his own state-of-the-art roaster using steel from the famous Forgemasters next door.

46-47 Wilson St, Neepsend, Sheffield S3 8DD
07885 445315
0114 2015815
frazerscoffeeroasters
@gmail.com
frazerscoffeeroasters.
co.uk

Every coffee roasted since 2016 has been made with that homemade roaster, a machine imbued with self-determined graft and a genuine love for the craft of coffee-making. Today, Frazer's Coffee is an established local brand with a strong focus on supporting direct trade, building stronger connections with farmers across the globe and ensuring the stories behind each bean are told.

GOO DESIGN

Matt Cockayne (known to most as Goo Design) not only illustrated the cover of this very book but he's also well known for his range of local landmark inspired illustrations, with Henderson's Relish a particularly striking source of inspiration.

Tell us about your business and how you started?

Back in 2013 I was working as a graphic designer at a printer in Chesterfield. I'd just moved into a new house and I wanted to bring a pinch of Sheffield to it, so I created a series of Henderson's Relish artworks. I was really pleased with them so I posted them to Hendos, who loved them and endorsed what I'd done, and since that day I have been selling art under the Goo label.

I now have four online shops selling Sheffield art, personalised football artworks as well as art for other cities around the world such as New York, Amsterdam and London.

What was the driving force for you to start your business?

Working for myself is what drives me, to be honest. I never really got on well with being employed and not having the freedom to do what I wanted to do; there's nothing more rewarding than working for myself and achieving my own goals.

Are there any other brands outside your sector that you are following at the moment?

I follow Thornbridge Brewery online and in person as I love their beers and branding. I did a live drawing in London recently at their tap takeover at the Tate Modern Art gallery and it was such an honour to be in such great company.

I also recently visited a bar in Kelham Island called the Parrot Club which I really liked so I drew the bar and they then asked if they could use the artwork for the label on their O'Hara's Rum, so I'm looking forward to seeing the new bottle launch.

I do mainly follow Sheffield based companies and believe in shopping locally and supporting the local economy.

What has your biggest achievement been so far?

I have achieved a lot in a short space of time from drawing my Herd elephant "Hendophant" to painting a mural on my favourite pub the Fat Cat, but my biggest achievement has to be launching the UK's first ever art banger rally which raised over £100k for Sheffield's youth homeless charity "Roundabout".

The rally went from Sheffield to Monte Carlo and raised awareness about the youth homelessness issue in Sheffield and the money has gone on to support the charity to expand further into the South Yorkshire region. Seeing the charity thrive has been very humbling and something I am extremely proud of.

goo-design.myshopify.com

ALMOST HOME KIDS
BY MATT COCKAYNE

There's nothing more rewarding than working for myself and achieving my own goals.

THE GREAT ESCAPE GAME

The Great Escape Game has seen whirlwind success since it was established by Hannah Duraid in 2015, branching out to other sites, creating innovative new experiences and attracting lots of attention from fans, families and celebrities across the country.

Sheffield's highly popular escape room attraction, The Great Escape Game, was founded by Hannah Duraid in 2015. Teams try to escape from their chosen adventure within a time limit using puzzles and clues, not unlike TV show The Crystal Maze. Hannah had first tried one while on holiday in Asia, and found that the comparison between this and the newly emerging UK market was vast, making it an opportunity too good to miss.

Running her new venture alongside PGCE teacher training, 16 hour days weren't uncommon. But thanks to almost immediate success, Hannah built a team to support their expansion into Leeds a year later, a newer site in Sheffield a year after that, and most recently an experience at The Royal Armouries Museum. Amongst these venues, Hannah has pushed the boundaries, creating a whole new social experience and filling the venue with a variety of multi-award-winning escape adventures.

These experiences include technologically advanced games and Hollywood-style sets, with themes that range from submarine warfare to abduction. The difficulty levels vary from beginner-friendly to challenging, so there's something for everyone, from families and birthday parties to groups of friends and date nights. Both venues now boast bars serving a selection of food and drink, and all lounge areas are open to the public, allowing players to chat about their adventures together while enjoying the free-of-charge retro arcades, consoles and board games on offer.

When the coronavirus pandemic hit, all sites were closed completely. Since then, the team has been drastically reduced and Hannah is much more hands-on again. "It's a great opportunity to get new insights while we're developing our new magical escape game, which will be launched early 2021," she says. The Sheffield venue can also be hired out privately, so The Great Escape Game is a perfect setting for celebrating occasions with something a little different that provides an opportunity to bond, put phones down and enjoy an adrenaline-fuelled afternoon. For anyone who loves puzzles, games and racing against the clock, this is the place to be!

The Great Escape Game
St James House, Gen 2:
Vicar Lane,
Sheffield S1 2EX
0330 088 3032

thegreatescapegame.co.uk
Twitter @_tgeg
Insta @thegreatescapegame
Tiktok @greatescapegame
Facebook: EscapeSheffield

INDEPENDENT SHEFFIELD

Breaking away from the chains, Independent Sheffield is on a mission to unearth hidden gems and link up with all those places that make Sheffield special.

From unsung heroes to the top dogs and everything in between, showcasing these venues and the incredible people behind them is what Independent Sheffield is all about.

"We have always been passionate about supporting local retailers in preference of larger franchised chains and with Independent Sheffield, we feel we can use our platform to spread the word about what this beautiful city has to offer, and create a community where we can all support each other. Especially now, when it's more important than ever to help these small businesses stay afloat through these strenuous times."

The Independent Sheffield membership card offers the opportunity to get rewarded for shopping local, and gives you exclusive access to an entire year's worth of discounts at all your favourite local indies. Over 50 venues have already joined the roster and Independent Sheffield hopes to double that amount by the end of 2021, so cardholders can make huge savings while supporting independents.

Social media is the best place to find out more, with regular content in the form of news, discounts, competitions, aesthetically pleasing photography, and memes!

Independent Sheffield Venues

Grazie
Macpot
Birdhouse Kitchen
Butcher & Catch
Eve Kitchen
Hygge Coffee Shop
EDO Sushi
Pom Kitchen
Steamyard
Kelham Wine Bar
Couch
Alyssum Café
The Cabin
Wildwood
Italia Uno
The Tramshed

Craft & Dough
Picture House Social
Homemade by Thelma's
The Milestone
Graze Inn
Tabby Teas
Cocoa Wonderland
Made by Jonty
The Beer Engine
The Leadmill
Trapeze Kids
Sinclairs
Sheffield Skincare Company
Frankly My Deer
Moonko
Turner's Beer Bottle Shop

Independent Sheffield
independent-sheffield.
co.uk
Instagram and Twitter: @
indpndntshef
Facebook: Independent
Sheffield

INDIE CATALOGUE

Sheffielders, illustrator & animator Emily Redfearn and web developer Jake Scales, responded to the COVID pandemic and subsequent lockdowns creatively, by creating Indie Catalogue to spread the word about hidden gems in the world of independents.

Indie Catalogue is a website entirely devoted to making shopping with independents online easier. Founders Emily and Jake want to help make indie businesses and makers more visible by linking customers directly to their online shops and websites. Customers are able to search through hundreds of businesses filtered by region and product type, all made by someone that cares.

They started the platform because they found that it was hard to find many independent sellers other than through word of mouth, especially if you are relatively unestablished or have an independent website. The initial goal was to help indies receive more sales in the run up to Christmas 2020 during the pandemic.

Emily created the identity and illustration for Indie Catalogue. She's a freelance illustrator, animator and designer born and raised in Sheffield. Her work varies across animated GIFs, video animations, advertising, branding, book covers and more. A key part of Emily's work is her bold use of colour, which is integral to her illustrations and creative process.

Sheffield-based organisations she has worked with include Printed By Us, who sell screen prints and operate workshops to teach vulnerable people the craft of hand screen printing. She has collaborated with the food court Terrace Goods, based in Orchard Square, on their rebrand, design and interior artwork. Emily has produced the animated GIFS that The Leadmill use on their social media channels, and has also previously lectured part time at Hallam University.

Jake is a web developer based in Sheffield. He has built and designed the entire website for Indie Catalogue. Jake came to Sheffield back in 2012 for university and fell in love with the city and everything in and around it. He graduated in 2015 and has since been working for multiple creative agencies as a web developer. In the past Jake has volunteered his time to help Cavendish Cancer Care (a local charity) revamp their existing site, along with raising money for them by running the Sheffield Half Marathon.

Indie Catalogue
indiecatalogue.co.uk
Follow us on social media
@IndieCatalogue

Emily Redfearn
emilyredfearn.co.uk
Follow her on Twitter and
Instagram @emredfearn

Jake Scales
www.jakescales.com

ITALIANEESE

If you are a cheese lover look no further than Italianeese, Sheffield's indie snack haven ready to bring a smile to your face and warmth to the soul.

Italianeese
Pick up and Delivery address at Sheffield Made: Unit 6, 92 Burton Road, Neepsend, Sheffield, S3 8BX
0114 360 3220
hello@italianeese.com
italianeese.com
@italianeese

Cheese is the staple for Italianeese, and it is this richness paired with onions encased in a deliciously fluffy bread roll that makes it a real winner. It's a great alternative to pizza and perfect for picnics and snacks – It's fluffy, it's cheesy, it's Italianeese!

The dough is always vegan, with a choice between either vegan or vegetarian cheese. Then it's all baked and topped with vegan or non-vegan egg wash and organic oregano, producing a luxurious aroma ready to tease the taste buds.

Italianeese also takes inspiration from the community, adapting the recipe so that they are something that can be made locally. It's a small operation full of personal touches, with a focus on sustainability and community; they source organic products and collaborate with Sheffield Made, a delivery company which has become an online farmers' market, taking pride in working with local producers. Along with Sheffield Made, local delivery apps deliver these freshly baked goodies door to door, and Italianeese are proud to be interacting with clients at home, aiming to provide a sustainable service online to cater for the hungry customer.

LOCKSLEY DISTILLING CO.

An idea formulated in the Big Apple and fermented here in the Steel City, Locksley Distilling Co. produce a range of high-quality artisan beverages including their famous Sir Robin of Locksley gin.

After living in New York for eight years, husband and wife team John Cherry and Cynthia King moved to Sheffield in 2013 to start their own craft distillery. Sheffielder John had worked in the wine and spirits industry for two decades, with experience ranging across both hospitality and retail, seeing first-hand the craft brewing scene blossom Stateside and eventually travel across the pond. After meeting some inspirational distillers in the US, he thought that craft distilleries could be the next big thing and together they began laying the groundwork for the company.

Incorporated in January 2013, Locksley Distilling Co. launched its first gin a year later. Named after folklore legend Robin Hood, said to hail from the Locksley (or Loxley) area of Sheffield, Sir Robin of Locksley was one of the first off-dry style gins on the market, with a distinctly sweet taste and notes of elderflower, pink grapefruit and liquorice. It was an instant hit and to this day remains the company's best-selling product.

As predicted, craft spirits followed craft beers and the 'ginaissance' ensued, with the number of UK distilleries doubling between 2015 and 2020. "The first few years were pretty crazy," says Cynthia. "We initially thought we'd be focusing on export, but the gin scene took off here and we toured the UK with the first ever nationwide gin festival, while John was catching flights to New York to try get it going over there. Our first gin we called a "sipping gin" – meaning you could sip it neat, which was quite unusual at the time, and it became our flagship product."

Lockley Distilling Co. has been based at Portland Works since 2014, a Grade II*-listed building home to a lively community of independent artists and small businesses. Their ethos is fairly straightforward: high-quality beverages with no shortcuts taken and a commitment towards working in an ethical and environmentally friendly way. Local produce is used, organic botanicals are sourced, fair prices are paid, waste is actively reduced, and they actively choose to work with smaller independent retailers in Sheffield when it comes to stocking their products.

A local approach is also adopted when it comes to collaborations, having worked with the likes of Thornbridge Brewery, Bullion Craft Chocolate and Foundry Coffee Roasters, amongst others. Cynthia explains that in what has been a challenging year, Locksley, along with so many other independent businesses, have had to adapt and take things online. "We'll be doing virtual gin tastings and masterclasses, setting up online calls and zoom parties where people can still experience what we offer and learn about the making process. Obviously, things will look a little different this Christmas, but we are working to make sure we can still provide people with some quality products and a good time."

Locksley Distilling Co.
Portland Works, Randall St, S2 4SJ
0114 249 0359
locksleydistilling.com

MEZE PUBLISHING

Meze Publishing are Sheffield's leading specialist cook book publisher. As a small independent business ourselves, we were delighted to work in collaboration with our sister company, Exposed Magazine, to bring this collection of brilliant businesses together and celebrate the city's creativity with The Little Book of Sheffield.

Meze Publishing was formed in 2013 by three publishing professionals: Paul Cocker, Nick Hallam and Phil Turner. Since then, we have worked with Michelin-starred chefs, won Best Newcomer at the Independent Publishing Guild Awards and moved into our own office development. During this time, we've grown as a team and developed as a business, publishing over 80 titles for chefs and cooks throughout the country. Throughout all of this we've maintained our core ethos of producing high quality, beautiful books that sell.

Our first publication and runaway success was The Sheffield Cook Book back in 2014, which showcased a diverse range of independent food and drink businesses throughout the city and sold over 12,000 copies. The 'Get Stuck In' series followed in its footsteps with another 42 cook books, always showcasing the area's best indies, that cover most of the UK from Edinburgh to Cornwall, and we even branched out into mainland Europe with Den Haag and Amsterdam editions. Alongside our regional titles, Meze works with chefs, cooks, foodies and producers to create tailored cook books full of great stories, delicious recipes and stunning photography.

These publications have included Out Of My Tree by Daniel Clifford, chef patron of the two-Michelin-starred Midsummer House in Cambridge, and of course Strong & Northern with Sheffield's own foodie pride and joy, Henderson's Relish. We've worked with lots of local photographers, designers, illustrators, producers, and independent businesses along the way including PJ Taste, The Milestone Group and Make No Bones. Recently, we have also produced several books with charities, donating some of the profits from book sales back to the organisations, including Whirlow Hall Farm in Sheffield.

We have a small but dedicated team who all love food as much as our clients do, and relish the opportunity to work with the city's hidden gems, golden oldies, new arrivals and everyone in between on our various local projects and publications. We hope you enjoy The Little Book of Sheffield and will continue to champion our hometown's eclectic and inspiring independent culture long into the future.

Meze Publishing
Unit 1B, 2 Kelham Square,
Kelham Riverside,
Sheffield S3 8SD
0114 275 7709
mezepublishing.co.uk
info@
mezepublishing.co.uk
Insta: @mezepublishing

STRONG &
NORTHERN

STRONG & NORTHERN

THE HENDERSON'S RELISH COOK BOOK

STRONG & NORTHERN
STRONG & NORTHERN

OUT of my TREE
MIDSUMMER HOUSE BY DANIEL CLIFFORD

MITCHELL'S WINE MERCHANTS

Mitchell's Wine Merchants is an integral part of Sheffield, and their name has been known in Meadowhead for 85 years.

The store is run by John Mitchell and his daughter Frankie, who is the third generation of the family to run the store. Mitchell's grandfather was a publican at the George IV pub on Infirmary Road when he sent his son to Henry Fanshawe School in Dronfield. On his journey, a row of shops caught his eye in Meadowhead, and he went to be an apprentice butcher before owning his own butchers in 1935. In 1961, the family moved out of the living quarters in the shop, and Mitchell's father refurbished it into a beer off, later to become the wine merchants it is today, opening a new chapter in the life of the family.

Sheffield runs in Mitchell's blood, and the family really are built into the brickwork of the city. His great-grandfather, Henry Sampson, owned a pub back in the 1860s called Adelphi, which was where Sheffield Wednesday and Yorkshire Cricket were founded. The pub was pulled down in 1970 and replaced with the famous Crucible theatre, and even further back down the line of Steel City ancestors is Thomas Boulsover who invented Sheffield plate.

The merchants are highly regarded throughout Yorkshire, achieving a tremendous number of awards including Wine Merchant of the Year twice, as well as the same in the beer and spirit categories. They showcase some of the finest selections in the UK at an affordable price. The heavily stocked cabinets feature more than 1000 wines, 600 whiskeys and 1000 beers in total – 500 of which are craft beers! It also holds an impressive selection of Havana cigars and is the second largest retailer of these in the north. With so much to choose from there really is something for everyone, so why not pop by to try something new?

From starting as a small family business to most recently delivering far and wide, Mitchell's continues to achieve. Sending out 100 deliveries a week both locally and nationally, they have made it easier for everyone to try their wines, bringing the fun straight to your doorstep. With such an illustrious history and unique array of products, Mitchell's place in Sheffield is firmly secured, and the proud owner hopes that the family will continue to bring one of life's greatest pleasures to the locals of the city for many more generations to come.

Mitchell's Wine
Merchants Ltd
354 Meadowhead,
Sheffield, S8 7UJ
0114 274 5587
info@mitchellswine.co.uk
@mitchellswine
mitchellswine.co.uk

WINES

GONZALEZ BYASS
BRISTOL MILK
SHERRY

GONZALEZ BYASS
MEDIUM DRY
SHERRY

EST 1935
IN SHEFFIELD **MITCHELLS WINES** EST 1935
IN SHEFFIELD

HAVANA CIGAR
SPECIALIST

TRIPPET LANE S1

MOSS VALLEY FINE MEATS

Stephen Thompson of Moss Valley Fine Meats, a local producer based in North East Derbyshire, talks about his proudest achievements on the farm and the importance of supporting local...

The farm has been in your family for a long time; who's the next in line to take up the Moss Valley mantle?

Oliver, our eldest son, works on the farm alongside his own business. Slowly but surely, he's taking over from Karen and I, which means there's a fifth generation coming forward, hopefully! We've worked this farm for over 100 years, so there's a lot of important family ties here.

What's most important to you about how the business is run?

High welfare for our animals is a big thing. We keep the pigs very healthy, and have one of the lowest rates of antibiotic use in the country, which is paramount for human health too. It is about better quality produce, but also about doing it right for the animals.

Your butchery is carbon neutral, so sustainability must be a key focus too?

Yes, we have a biomass boiler at the butchery and we reckon the whole farm is carbon neutral by this point. We use wind turbines and solar panels, sell the woodchip we produce to power plants... anything to try and leave things better than they were. Our pig muck goes back onto the fields to grow the crops that feed the pigs, so we don't need to introduce more chemicals – no phosphorus or potash, only a small amount of nitrogen – which creates a closed and a healthier nutrient cycle.

And what do you produce on site in the butchery?

We try to offer the biggest range of pork produce we can: burgers, joints, bacon, sausages... in the very near future we're expanding the butchery and will soon be able to do cooked meats as well such as hams and black pudding, so watch this space.

What would you say is Moss Valley Fine Meats' highest achievement?

We won Outstanding Achievement from the National Pig Association and we're up for Pig Producer of the Year from Farmer's Weekly in 2020, fingers crossed! We're also very proud that local restaurants want to work with us. Despite the pandemic, we've not lost any customers so it's reassuring to think that they're all hanging in there, and will hopefully come out of the other side by supporting each other.

AVAILABLE ON CITY GRAB

Moss Valley Fine Meats, Lightwood Lane, Sheffield S8 8BG // 0114 2399922 / 07976434206
// www.mossvalleyfinemeats.co.uk // info@mossvalleyfinemeats.co.uk

MAKERS // The Little Book of Sheffield

MOSS VALLEY PORK COLLAR WITH NAM JIM JAEW BY LUKE FRENCH, JÖRO

Barbecuing over fire is my favourite way to cook vegetables, fish and meat, but if you can't be bothered or don't have a barbecue, then a pan and the oven will do just fine for this pork. I serve it with a Thai-style dipping sauce that goes so well with grilled meats. I have been working with Stephen and the guys at Moss Valley Fine Meats since the beginning at Jöro, and I truly believe their pigs are among some of the best in the UK.

Jöro Restaurant
0.2-0.5 Krynkl,
294, Shalesmoor,
Sheffield
S3 8US
0114 299 1539

Preparation time: 20 minutes plus 12 hours marinating | Cooking time: 1 hour | Serves 8

This is a great dish to share with your friends and family, super simple to prepare and cook, and so delicious!

For the nam jim jaew
1 tbsp white rice
25g sustainable palm sugar
20g light soy sauce
20g tamarind paste
60g fish sauce (we use Squid brand)
15g fresh coriander, leaves and stalks washed and chopped
3 kaffir lime leaves, finely chopped
2g dried chilli flakes
1 fresh lime, juiced
1 spring onion, washed and chopped
1 shallot, peeled and sliced

For the pork
1 boned & rolled Moss Valley pork collar
60g golden caster sugar
25g table salt
15g smoked sea salt & 5g pink salt
8g chicken stock granules
5g Chinese five spice
2g onion powder
2g smoked paprika
1g dried chilli flakes
1g each white & black peppercorns
10g black treacle
5 cloves of garlic, peeled and crushed
1 tsp lemongrass and ginger paste

For the nam jim jaew

First, toast the white rice in a hot dry pan, then let it cool and grind to a powder with a pestle and mortar. Place the palm sugar in the pestle and mix in the soy sauce, tamarind and fish sauce to make a loose paste. Add the rest of the ingredients and stir to combine. Refrigerate; it will keep in an airtight container for 2 weeks.

For the pork

Blend all of the dry ingredients to a powder, then stir in the treacle, crushed garlic and lemongrass paste. Rub this mixture all over the pork collar, then place it into a sterile dish, cover with cling film and refrigerate for 12 hours or overnight.

Rinse the marinated pork under cold running water for 5 minutes, then pat dry and leave covered in a sterile dish for at least 1 hour at room temperature before cooking. Preheat a heavy-based pan with a good glug of cooking oil in. Carefully place the pork into the hot oil and keep turning until all sides are heavily coloured and caramelised. Remove from the pan and place it on a tray to rest.

Preheat a charcoal-fuelled barbecue and carefully place the pork over the hot coals, turning it with a pair of flame-proof tongs every 15 seconds, for 3 to 5 minutes, until it is very dark and has a good bark on it. Meanwhile, preheat your oven to 140°c. Transfer the pork from the barbecue into an ovenproof roasting tray and cook in the oven for 40 minutes. Remove from the oven and allow to rest for 20 minutes on a wire rack. The core temperature of the pork should be around 55°c.

Once rested, slice the pork lengthways down the middle and then carve each length into nice chunky slices, place in a serving dish and serve it family-style, with the nam jim jaew dipping sauce on the side. This dish is great served with some bowls of salads, noodles and rice.

THE SHEFFIELD GUIDE

A longstanding advocate of the city's history and culture, James Hargreaves is the founder of The Sheffield Guide – an online platform dedicated to Steel City news, video content and merchandise.

A born-and-bred Sheffielder, James has worked as a marketing consultant for over 15 years, collaborating with many local businesses, brands and events across South Yorkshire.

Initially a hobby, The Sheffield Guide began as a way to showcase video content promoting everything the city has to offer. Local interest videos detailing the history of Kelham Island, highlighting hidden gems and exploring the city's underground rivers were uploaded to a YouTube channel and Facebook page, accumulating hundreds of thousands of views.

When the pandemic hit, James' work began to dry up and The Sheffield Guide became a new creative outlet, allowing him to put his experience in online marketing and a long-time love of illustration to good use. Having to shield from the virus, James was forced to put a hold on the videos and focus on fresh online content, eventually working on a series of sketches and designs promoting Sheffield culture in the shape of iconic buildings from past and present, much-loved local brands, and nods to musical heritage.

"Being a freelancer when the pandemic hit meant I fell through the cracks of government support, so I had to get creative," says James. "Lockdown gave me the opportunity to focus on my drawing again and I gravitated to what I know best – Sheffield's history, legacy and culture. I began with just eight designs, and I've been expanding the collection ever since."

There's now a vast range of products available to purchase on The Sheffield Guide website. You'll find prints, mugs, t-shirts, hoodies, towels, cushions, facemasks and more – all embodying a distinct Steel City flavour and made with a strong ethos geared towards sustainability, right down to the plastic-free packaging.

Products such as the Jarvis Cocker 'Pulp Fiction' print have been sent around the globe, while homages to Tinsley Towers and the Henderson's Relish factory have naturally been a great success closer to home. James is keen get back out and work on new video content when safe to do so, but in the meantime there's plenty more designs to come, and with new requests and ideas coming almost every week, he's certainly got his work cut out.

"There's an endless amount of stuff to draw! I need to keep making sure I've got time to keep the blog side of The Sheffield Guide running too, but I'm going to keep adding to the product list and don't be surprised to see a few exciting collaborations coming soon!"

Visit The Sheffield Guide at: www.sheffieldguide.blog

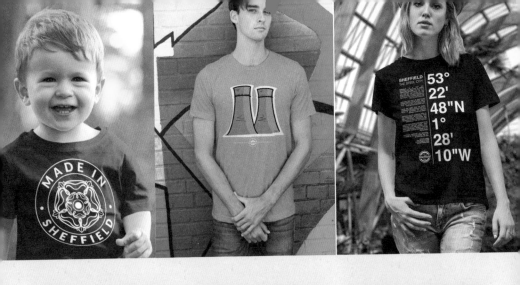

THE STEEL CITY STANDARD

The Steel City Standard, an online news outlet established in September 2020, compiles fresh and original content including local history, lifestyle, music, culture and current events to share news and experiences within the Sheffield community.

After graduating from The University of Sheffield in 2019 and taking a few months out, the creator realised that there was room for a newcomer in the city's media landscape, and soon rediscovered her love of writing by pairing it with something she loved equally: Sheffield. From the seeds of this idea, The Steel City Standard was founded, providing a space for different voices and perspectives in the news and media.

It also aims to offer opportunities and resources for budding journalists to find their voice. Volunteering to write for the news outlet gives contributors first-hand experience in the media, allowing those with journalistic ambitions to hone their skills and gain valuable experience. People of all ages and backgrounds are encouraged to provide content, including but not limited to students and young people, and the outlet is designed to appeal to a traditional audience while remaining open-minded and offering something that little bit different from the norm.

Covering everything and anything, bringing together a diverse range of news and articles is the foundation of what they do. There's no such thing as 'not our thing' for The Steel City Standard; content is welcomed as long as it's interesting, accurate and well written. Any good ideas are considered and don't have to be related to Sheffield, though local news will always have a place in the outlet by name and by nature.

The young independent enterprise may be small, but has big ambitions for future projects in the hope of making a real impact on the city. If you are interested in writing for the online news outlet, visit the website and social media listed below.

The Steel City Standard
www.steelcitystandard.com
steelcitystandard@gmail.com
Find us on LinkedIn, Facebook, Twitter and Instagram @ SteelCityStand

TRIPLE POINT

Triple Point Brewing Ltd is a brewery and bar located on Shoreham Street, just a short walk from Sheffield train station and its famous tap. Run by Mike and George Brook, a father and son duo who took over the brewery in November 2018, Triple Point has won awards for its brews which feature in popular venues across Sheffield and beyond.

Despite neither having worked in a brewery previously, George and Mike felt they couldn't turn down the serendipitous opportunity to launch Triple Point and give brewing a go when Mike's brother, a brewery owner himself, first flagged the plot. It came at the right time for the pair, as Mike was taking a sabbatical from work and George was contemplating moving to London for a "boring grad job". However, after trying some of the beer the existing kit produced, they knew it was an opportunity not to be missed. With master brewer Alex in tow, they took on the challenge of re-possessing and running a brewery and bar with no previous experience, and to great success!

Alongside their favoured lagers and beers, Triple Point Brewing is also home to the popular Twisted Burger Company. The natural pairing of burgers and beers makes the bar a prevalent spot for those seeking post-work replenishment, as well as weekend punters. They also boast a spacious outdoor area (something central Sheffield pubs are in need of) which acts as a perfect afternoon suntrap in the brighter months. However, regulars know that the best seats are inside, where you can gaze upon the spectacular brewing kit in all of its exposed glory.

Mike and George pride themselves on the quality of their beers, which is why they keep them in their tanks for as long as possible to be served tank-to-glass, ensuring freshness. Recently, the brewery's Parkin Amber Ale has been a real favourite amongst customers, and the team are brewing up new treats in time for Christmas, including 'Substantial Meal', a Session IPA from which £1 of every can goes towards combatting food poverty, and a new pour made in collaboration with Kelham Island's Bullion Chocolate.

Triple Point Brewing is offering take-away options for both beers and burgers during the uncertain period of lockdown closure ahead. The online shop is also open, and with options from cans to kegs, casks to cases, it's a great place to do some Christmas shopping. Just remember to get a few cans for yourself, too!

THE VILLAGE SCREEN

From hosting incredible pop-up cinemas on car park rooftops in Sheffield to caves in Derbyshire, as well as adapting to offer Drive-in cinemas in 2020, the team behind The Village Screen has hosted some of the most unique events in the city since establishing itself in 2015. Despite a tricky year for live events in 2020, Claire Atkinson, Eamonn Hunt and Emily Dexter have adapted and continued to host truly special events for the people of Sheffield.

Despite only forming in 2015, The Village Screen feels like it has been part of the furniture in Sheffield for much longer. Perhaps it's due to the constantly sold-out events, rave reviews and spectacular locations, or the hard work that goes on behind the scenes to make each event extra special.

Co-founder Claire Atkinson gives her verdict: "We look after our customers and we are passionate about creating fantastic experiences in unique locations. I think it's the little touches that make our events – epic lighting, fun décor, and our incredible cinema equipment which we've invested hugely in. We have a fantastic team of audio visual specialists who ensure every event is seamless. People notice the small details we put in but they wouldn't come back if the picture and sound quality wasn't excellent. We focus on getting the basics right too."

As for why The Village Screen has become so popular, co-founder Eamonn says The Village Screen has a great personality. "We are very clear about the way our events are stylised and the way that our customers experience our events. We are an independent company that employs local people and supports local businesses, breweries and food vendors, and we've also helped one or two new ventures to get off the ground too. Our customers see what we do, they appreciate that we are open, friendly and supportive, and in return, they support us."

Production manager Emily Dexter agrees. "We show a lot of personality through our marketing, so we get to know our customers and they get to know us! This has allowed us to build a loyal following of people who get what we are about. We always go the extra mile too, whether that be with theming to make the experience the best it can be, or with keeping our customers happy. It's this that makes our events truly unique."

When asked about their favourite Village Screen events, Emily chooses one at the Peak Cavern: "It has to be Jurassic Park at the Peak Cavern! The cave itself is a jaw-dropping location but throw in a classic film, epic street food and live music and you have yourself something amazing! Jurassic Park brings back floods of nostalgia for me and watching it inside a cave with the backdrop of the sun setting over Castleton is such an incredible experience."

With a clearly talented team and a knack for putting on fantastic events, we look forward to seeing what they have to offer in 2021 and beyond.

The Village Screen
01143603503
@thevillagescreen
thevillagescreen.com

THE VILLAGE GREEN EVENTS CO.

The team behind The Village Screen pop-up cinema in Sheffield also launched The Village Green Events Co. in 2015 – a creative events production company that helps to plan weddings and celebration events, as well as private pop-up cinema events for corporate organisations, product launches, award ceremonies and everything in between.

When Claire Atkinson, Eamonn Hunt and Emily Dexter are not delivering Village Screen events, they are working to transform often blank-canvas spaces into stunning wedding and events venues, and have some enviable and varied clients including Historic England, Arla Foods, the NHS and St Luke's Hospice.

With 40 years industry experience, Eamonn believes the team's strength comes from delivering more than what their clients think is possible. He has worked with global brands, on small scale theatre tours, the Olympic Games, and international stadium tours; he understands how to make any venue work and how to build the best possible team to do it.

Claire honed her craft working as a lawyer which made her "incredibly detail-focused" before looking after corporate sponsors at the Science Museum in London. "We believe in not having a one-size-fits all approach. We work with clients on all kinds of budgets and we love the opportunity to bring their vision to life. I personally love working on weddings because we can really get to know a couple and weave their personality throughout the planning process."

Emily adds: "All of our weddings are beautiful but we love the opportunity to be imaginative. We've helped a tennis-loving couple plan a wedding on a tennis court and a couple who love 50's vintage plan a retro/pirate themed wedding at Trafalgar Warehouse. We also helped the NHS plan a fantastic Sheffield-themed conference at Peddler in Sheffield last year. We were one of the first companies to plan a wedding at Peddler too, which has now become a favourite location of ours because it is a completely blank canvas."

"We believe in pushing the boundaries when it comes to creativity and imaginative planning," says Eamonn. "We're very comfortable working on on all styles of weddings and events. We work on weddings for couples on tight budgets, as well as ones where the budget would buy you a house. A recent wedding involved the client taking over a whole country estate that they married in, and I'm currently organising a wedding that has involved conversations with the local council about introducing a temporary one-way traffic system to deal with the huge influx of guests over what will be a four day event."

The Village Green Events Co. offers a full or partial planning service. They also help couples who want to plan their own wedding by offering a set-up and on-the-day wedding coordination service, perfect for dry hire venues or marquee weddings. They also have a treasure trove of hire items from deckchairs, to outdoor furniture, lighting, PA systems and more.

The Village Green Events Co.
01143603503
@villagegreenevents
thevillagegreenevents.com

YEE KWAN ICE CREAM

Drawing inspiration from East Asian culture, family-run artisan ice cream company Yee Kwan Ice Cream have created an award-winning product which comes in a variety of unique and exciting flavours. It was on a life-changing tour of Australasia that Yee Kwan and husband Anthony were inspired by amazing flavours experienced in the bustling food markets, returning to the UK with a business idea that would eventually entice Dragons' Den star Deborah Meaden to invest in the company and help bring the dream to life. Here, Yee Kwan tells us a bit more about their story so far...

Can you tell us a bit about the ethos behind the Yee Kwan brand?

Our ethos is to create unique ice cream, sorbet and desserts, with flavours that are inspired by our exotic travels and Chinese heritage. The most important thing is to bring smiles and happy memories to all of our customers.

A big boost came following a successful pitch on Dragons' Den, which saw Deborah Meaden investing in the company. How would you describe that experience?

The Dragons' Den pitch was terrifying; I was so nervous on the day of filming! It was a valuable experience for me and I learned a lot from Deborah Meaden, which has really supported the growth of our business.

What is it like working as part of the Sheffield food and producers community?

We're so lucky to be part of such a welcoming and collaborative bunch of food producers and independents in Sheffield. We've been established for over 10 years and I'm all about supporting and helping new businesses and entrepreneurs on their journey, offering any advice I can give so they don't make the same mistakes as me!

How do you source the ingredients for your standout flavours?

It is really important to us to source the best quality ingredients we can find. We can't source certain ingredients locally, such as the Japanese matcha, miso or black sesame seeds, but all the milk and cream we use is sourced from a farmer in Tideswell.

What do you think has helped set Yee Kwan apart and become so popular, especially here in Sheffield?

I'd say it's a mixture of things: the quality of our flavours, the big ice cream cones we serve at the local events we attend, and our service with a smile.

What is your proudest achievement to date?

There have been so many, and I don't think I stop to celebrate the wins as much as I should. I guess it has to be seeing our products on the shelves in supermarkets in China, Abu Dhabi, Dubai and on the menus of Wagamama. That's a special feeling.

AVAILABLE ON CITY GRAB

yeekwan.com // @yeekwanicecream // 0114 327 7949 // @YeeKwanIceCream

THE YORKSHIRE CANDLE COMPANY

We are The Yorkshire Candle Company (if you're in Sheffield then you may know us as The Sheffield Candle Company). We are based just outside the heart of the city of Sheffield, in Attercliffe. Our workshop and offices are inside an old industrial building which has been redeveloped and this is where the magic happens.

We handcraft all of our own products at our workshop. Every aspect of our production process is done by hand, from securing the wick, to mixing our fragrance, to pouring our candles. All of our products are produced in small batches and this means we are able to consistently create products of the highest quality.

Our materials are responsibly sourced, we only ever use trusted suppliers who are known within the industry and who share our ethical and responsible standpoint. The wax we use is 100% natural soy wax, which is grown on responsible and certified European farmland, and this is an environmentally friendly alternative to traditional candle waxes. Our wicks are created with natural cotton and our fragrances encompass both naturally occurring ingredients and other supplementary ingredients.

So you may be asking yourself where did all this begin? Well in 2014 James, the founder of The Yorkshire Candle Company, was growing an idea which revolved around fragrance and personal experience. Originally we set up as The Sheffield Candle Company and our landmark-inspired products were developed to not only smell nice but also evoke memories which were personal to each individual using our products. This fragrance range then expanded to include other scents such as Dark Roast Coffee and Plum & Rhubarb.

As we developed and began to expand, we wanted to open our products and the experience of them to a wider audience, and this is when The Yorkshire Candle Company was born. We continued with our landmark-inspired candles with popular scents such as The Yorkshire Dales and Whitby Bay. We are always working on new scents and as of September 2020 we launched our newest landmark fragrance, Peak District, as well as some other scents for our range which include Fig & Bramble.

Behind the scenes we are always working to expand the range of products which we are able to offer and soon we are hoping to launch a range of reed diffusers, room mists and other products which are still in development.

Over the last five years we have been shown so much love and support by the people of Sheffield and Yorkshire. I want to take this opportunity to say thank you to everyone who has ever purchased from us, to everyone who may purchase in the future and lastly from our great team (Team Candle!), we hope you enjoy your candles!

The Yorkshire Candle Company
0114 3272323
info@
theyorkshirecandleco.
co.uk
theyorkshirecandleco.
co.uk

MAKERS

The 'best of the rest' of our city's creatives.

CAST // experiencecast.com
A bespoke jewellery making business, CAST often team up with local venues to create a unique social experience. Chat amongst pals whilst crafting your jewellery, then CAST does the rest and delivers high quality rings, necklaces and bracelets in the post.

Colours of Sheffield //
coloursofsheffield.etsy.com
Providing some uplifting splashes of colour during what has often felt like a grey few months in 2020, Mary Tear is on an aesthetically pleasing mission to match up various pieces of Steel City with her selection of Pantone cards. Head over to her online shop to see some iconic Sheffield landmarks matched nicely with her cards.

Stoneface Creative // stonefacecreative.com
Andrew Vickers, also known locally as Stoneface Creative, heads up his outdoor gallery in Storrs Wood, Stannington. A truly unique Sheffield artist, Stoneface Creative's sculptures are open for the public to view anytime, in what the artist calls his 'green cathedral'.

La Biblioteka // labiblioteka.co
Independent book shop based inside the Kommune food hall and social space. Some real gems to be picked up here and online with limited edition magazines, best-selling novels and publications by local authors.

Yorkshire Artspace // artspace.org.uk
Established in 1977 by art graduates, Yorkshire Artspace was one of the first studio groups developed outside of London, where the studio movement began in the late 1960s. Since then, it's grown to become one of the largest and most established studio providers in the UK.

Otis Mensah // otismensah.com
The young rapper/story-teller made history in 2018 as he became Sheffield's first Poet Laureate. Otis has been making waves for years, representing the Steel City at Glastonbury, on the BBC and Berlin's Poetry Meets Hip Hop.

Warda Yassin // wardayassin.me
Award-winning poet and secondary school teacher, Warda Yassin recently took on the mantle of the city's Poet Laureate. Whilst running the Mixing Roots project for young people of colour with Hive South Yorkshire, Warda has also had her poetry published in places like The North, Magma and Oxford Poetry.

RETAILERS

THE BARE ALTERNATIVE

The Bare Alternative is a zero waste and refill shop providing affordable, plastic-free shopping to Abbeydale Road and the surrounding areas.

Established in November 2018, The Bare Alternative soon outgrew its initial premises due to the popularity of the refill concept and a positive reception from the local community around Abbeydale Road. In November 2020, the shop moved into a new home, becoming Sheffield's largest retailer of refill and eco-friendly products. The extra space has given the team an opportunity to add different product ranges and increase the choice of refill items. Stocking up your pantry with the best quality produce of those harder to refill items is now possible, and The Bare Alternative is always listening to customer feedback to provide more items that are hard to buy without large amounts of non-recyclable packaging.

One of the shop's aims is to make packaging-free shopping accessible for all. They offer a wide selection of wholefoods and cooking ingredients for making healthy meals, alongside a range of natural cleaning products, everyday sustainable alternatives such as bamboo toothbrushes and steel straws, and much more, to help everyone reduce waste and live a more sustainable lifestyle. Many items are provided free from packaging, so shoppers need to remember to bring their own containers, or BYOC!

Owner Mathew Reynolds says: "With the known issues of plastic pollution in our rivers and oceans, it is so important that we look for ways of preventing this from happening. At the end of our first year of trading, we helped the local community save just short of 4000kg of plastic waste, compared to buying pre-packaged, and we've been working hard to find new suppliers and products to increase that number."

The Bare Alternative is founded on an ethical and eco-friendly ethos, focused on creating ways to reduce waste and prevent the need for unnecessary packaging, which is then sent to landfill or incinerators. Shopping this way also means you can buy only what you need, keeping costs down and reducing food waste too. The shop's team put a lot of effort into researching the products they sell, ensuring that they fit within this ethos so customers can be confident they are making a difference. This approach helps to reduce every shopper's environmental impact, and ultimately tackle the climate crisis with positive action.

The Bare Alternative
332 Abbeydale Road,
Sheffield, S7 1FN
07422405166
barealternative.co.uk

BESPOKE BLINDS & POLES

With 50 years' experience in the industry, husband and wife team Maxine and Neil Hayter are owners of one of the oldest independent blind companies in the city. After cutting their teeth at the famous Cole Brothers department store in the city centre, the couple decided to open their own premises in 2007. We spoke to Maxine Hayter about the couple's journey so far...

How did you come to open your own store?

From the age of 16, I joined Cole Brothers on a YTS scheme, and stayed there for 21 years. Working at Cole Brothers helped hugely in how to work and meet all types of people. It has always been a beacon for shopping in Sheffield, and you meet all sorts of life there. You look back at some of the people you crossed paths with and, just wow! As an aside, I met my husband Neil there. He was working on the departments as an estimator, and I was on the same department in sales. After a few career changes, in 2007, someone in the industry suggested to Neil we should start our own company because it was an under-represented area in Sheffield at that time. People always say to us, because we've worked in retail so long, that this was our dream, but it didn't really happen like that. We just found the premises, got started and 13 years later here we are!

That's literally like that famous Richard Hawley song...

Exactly that! We are Richard Hawley, we took his songs to heart.

And what does Bespoke Blinds & Poles offer?

Anything that covers a window; both inside and outside. Our best seller over the last couple of years has definitely been shutters. The biggest changes over the last few years have been improvements in child safety, and motorised products. Yes, if you want to tell your curtains to close, they will!

What's Neil's role in the business?

Neil is a problem solver, he goes into people's homes and he's got the knack of talking to people and helping them realise their vision. He's the creative side of the business in that respect. For us though, it's the customers that make everything worthwhile.

As lovers of all things Steel City, what's your favourite part of Sheffield?

Coming from Sheffield, you tend to take the outdoors stuff for granted, don't you? We've got dogs so love the scenery, and places like Millhouses Park and the Sheffield Botanical Gardens. We're often out in the Peaks and have spoken to people who've driven up from London because we're the first major climbing edges outside the capital, whereas we just nip over to Stanage like it's a normal thing. We're a bit older now, but we've loved working and socialising in Sheffield over the years. Starting work straight from school, and you're right in thinking the pub scene was amazing. Still is, although we're more into seeing bands than clubbing these days.

Bespoke Blinds & Poles
6 Hutcliffe Wood Road
Beauchief
S8 0EX
0114 236 3100
sheffieldblinds.co.uk

BESPOKE BLINDS & POLES

Tel. 0114 236 3100

www.sheffieldblinds.co.uk

THIS LUXAFLEX AWNING CAN BE OPERATED MANUALLY, REMOTELY, BY APP AND VOICE CONTROL

BIRD'S YARD

Having started life in Leeds, established by Michelle Walton (or 'Bird', hence the shop's name) in 2010, Bird's Yard is now a collection of over 70 of the best independent businesses and designers sourced locally and globally, housed on Chapel Walk in Sheffield city centre.

The shop offers a unique mix of products including jewellery, homewares, books, locally made preserves, t-shirts, artwork, skincare and babywear to name a few. Customers often say if they're looking for something for that hard to buy for person, they'll find it here! Sheffield features strongly too, with a range of products inspired by the city; you can find candles, prints, keyrings, bags, and even rubber ducks with a local theme!

Alongside Michelle, who leads the shop team, some of the designers housed in Bird's Yard help to run it, which is great for building relationships with customers. "It's rewarding to be able to offer customers new and sometimes bespoke designs, and always have a changing variety of stock, as well as continuing favourites, to offer something different. It adds a really personal touch to shopping and customers love meeting the designer of their purchase, and likewise for the designers to meet them," says Michelle.

They were thrilled to win the Championing Independents award in 2018 at the Shop Sheffield Awards, because that's the main aim of Bird's Yard, to provide local creatives with a place to establish and grow their business as well as connecting with a local audience. They are always on the hunt for exciting new talent too – details can be found on the website – to join their ever-expanding team.

2020 has seen huge investment in the website and online presence, allowing Bird's Yard to continue providing excellent face to face customer service for its loyal local following, while also being able to offer something for those farther afield, showcasing the full range of talent offered by Sheffield's independent artists, makers, designers, and creatives.

Bird's Yard
44 Chapel Walk,
Sheffield, S1 2PD
0114 2788709
@BirdsYardSheffield
birdsyard.co.uk

THE FAMOUS SHEFFIELD SHOP

The Famous Sheffield Shop has supported the craftmanship of the city since 1983 by sourcing the highest quality Sheffield-made products ready to sell locally to proud Sheffield customers and across the UK, as well as internationally.

The Famous Sheffield Shop sells the finest pewter, silver and steel ware made in Sheffield, demonstrating just how the Steel City got its famous name. They maintain a close relationship with all their suppliers, working with historical, family-owned businesses and emphasising just how important it is to be supporting independents. The team are proud to showcase only a handful of the excellent products they provide.

Joseph Rodgers was one of Sheffield's most famous knife makers, and he operated out of a building in Hawley Croft close to Sheffield Cathedral from 1682. The shop sells Rodgers' pocket knives with the Maltese Cross and Star trademark, as well as the George Wostenholm pocket and Bowie knife designs with his I*XL, 1787 trademark. After the battle of the Alamo in 1863, a Wolstenholm knife was reportedly found on Colonel James Bowie, and this design continues to be handmade in Sheffield today and is very popular with American customers as well as the locals.

William Whiteley's has been trading as a family-owned company for 258 years. Their range of high-quality scissors to fit all purposes are recognised worldwide. Arthur Price of Sheffield has produced cutlery of the highest quality since 1902, and The Famous Sheffield Shop sells their stainless-steel tableware to top restaurants and family homes across the globe.

The shop is not limited to knives and homeware; they also have a prestigious jewellery collection. Francis Howard silversmiths, founded in 1870, manufacture high quality jewellery and gifts suitable for every occasion. Wentworth Pewter is a family business founded in 1949, and their handcrafted flasks, tankards and other giftware are known for their quality and have graced the shelves of Tiffany and Liberty stores. Newer companies have also made their way to the forefront, including bracelets from Bailey and razors from Edwin Jagger. If you are looking for a dazzling gift for that special someone, look no further.

The Famous Sheffield Shop is more than just a retailer, having designed steak knives for some of the country's top restaurants. Being a much-loved fixture on Ecclesall Road, there is no doubt that regulars will continue to support Sheffield craftsmanship long into the future.

The Famous
Sheffield Shop
475 Ecclesall Road,
Sheffield, S11 8PP
0114 268 5701
sheffieldmade@gmail.com
sheffield-made.com
Facebook:
TheFamousSheffieldShop

FRESHMANS VINTAGE STORE

Freshmans Vintage Store is something of an institution when it comes to Sheffield's fashion scene, having sold the latest vintage trends for over two decades. Owner Louisa Froggatt talks about the trials and tribulations of running her well-loved shop with optimism and pride.

What's the best part of running such a longstanding business here in Sheffield?

We get three generations coming into the store, from ages 8 to 80, and people who shopped here as teenagers bring their children in, so that's quite special. Because we were the first vintage store in Sheffield, and had to survive before the internet, we're known mostly through word of mouth. You get such great comments from people; some come in a few times a week, some visit when they return to Sheffield because they remember us. I feel very proud of the shop's longevity.

You must have some great stories then?

We've had our fair share of famous faces! Freshmans has always had a really strong connection with the music scene here so all the up and coming bands tend to visit at some point. When we were in The Forum during the 1990s, Jarvis Cocker used to buy his velvet jackets from us, and we've still got Alex Turner's CV – the lead singer of the Arctic Monkeys – because he once applied for a job here. We've held gigs at the store before and there's a big one planned for March 2021 to celebrate 25 years of Freshmans.

A lot has changed during that time. What challenges have you faced and overcome?

The coronavirus pandemic obviously put a big dampener on 2020. We put lots of safety measures in place after the first lockdown, and had a positive attitude towards those changes, but it has been hard. So many events like festivals disappeared and we just haven't had the same volume of visitors. What we have got, though, is a really loyal following and we work hard to put that first because we love our customers.

What do you think people love about Freshmans that keeps them coming back?

People have told me that to them, we're more like a community than a store. I know lots of our customers by name, we're always going the extra mile to help people find the right products, and we pride ourselves on a really personal shopping experience. We recently launched a website so there's more opportunity to buy online too, but at heart we're an old-fashioned retailer that puts customers first.

Freshmans Vintage Store
6-8 Carver Street, Sheffield S1 4FS
freshmansvintagestore.com // 0114 272 8333 // freshmansvintagestore96@gmail.com

156

RETAILERS // **The Little Book of Sheffield**

GRAVEL PIT

A hub of the community and veritable gem of the indie retail scene, Gravel Pit has you covered when it comes to finding plants, handmade pots, prints, records and many other quirky products here in the Steel City.

Moving from Kelham Island to its current location on Abbeydale Road in 2018, owner Danny Mager has created a walk-in shrine to what he terms "the holy trinity of things in life – music, art and wellbeing."

With an onus on showcasing all things creative and unique, this emporium of delights contains three rooms housing everything from an enviable vinyl selection and various works from local artists, to interesting homeware pieces and independent publications.

Danny's love for horticulture is a driving force behind the business, the seeds of which (if you will forgive the pun) were sown when his brother provided him with a crash course in making glass terrariums. He quickly developed a knack for it and began selling his wares in small independent shops across the city, so the next step was concrete pots, which were also a hit, and eventually the opportunity to run his own retail space arose.

Today there aren't many plants Gravel Pit won't be able to source for you, and the pot room located at the back of the shop allows them to grow their own collection in-house. However, plants are just a small part of the offering here and they're keen to cater to a wide variety of tastes. "If somebody walks in that isn't into plants, then maybe they'll be into music, or artwork, or vice versa," Danny tells us. "It's all about creative things and an amalgamation of stuff that has inspired me over the years."

Community is at the heart of what they're all about, proud to be nestled amongst the ever-growing list of independents lined up along Abbeydale Road. A distinctly friendly, chilled-out vibe makes it a popular hangout for shoppers in the area; it's a place where genuine conversation and the building of relationships is prioritised over quick sales.

"We love it here and enjoy a symbiotic relationship with all the independent businesses in the area," says Danny. "There's a strong independent spirit and people come out to support it. People enjoy what the area had offer with all the restaurants, shops, bars and cafes – amazing places and cool spots which all offer something different. We're all about our ever-evolving range of curated plants, sourcing interesting products, and promoting the local arts scene."

Gravel Pit
329 Abbeydale Road,
Sheffield
S7 1FS
@gravelpithomeware
gravelpitshop.com

JAMESON'S GIFTS & ANTIQUES

Jameson's Gifts & Antiques is a treasure trove of unusual, quirky and individual items located above the tearoom of the same name.

The newest version of Jameson's Gifts & Antiques is more accessible than ever before and offers something a little bit different, from handmade greeting cards to vegan skincare. Having moved back into the same building as Jameson's Tearoom & Kitchens on the first floor the shop is now more closely linked with its sister business and shares the relaxed atmosphere. Customers can have a browse before enjoying afternoon tea, or pop upstairs after a coffee to find the perfect present, wrapping paper and card in one place.

The shop stocks a range of elegant yet contemporary gifts for children and adults, that are carefully chosen to be easy on the pocket, but not something you could pick up just anywhere. Jameson's have sold antiques in Sheffield since 1883 so these are still a big part of the offering too. Alongside quirky pieces of furniture, you'll find Jameson's own range of jams, curds and chutneys, 22 types of tea (including one blended especially for the shop and café, all by Northern Teas) and the Betty Hula range of vegan skincare products, to name just a few. Local artists and makers are very well represented, from handcrafted cards by the Sheffield-based Musker-Sherwood Designs to artwork by Anette Dyson. You can even have gifts personalised with the LoveLottie x range, which includes prints, cheeseboards, soft toys, glassware and cake toppers: these are also used by Jameson's in the tearoom.

Following the first lockdown due to the coronavirus pandemic, a leaky roof and then another lockdown in 2020, Jameson's Gifts & Antiques has diversified and adapted to overcome many hurdles. The crossover between the shop and the tearoom is one silver lining from a difficult year; as the café could no longer fill its full capacity due to social distancing restrictions, the gifts and antiques occupied the extra space which has brought the business more in sync. Gift vouchers for Jameson's Tearoom & Kitchens can be bought in the shop, and a 10% discount is offered when customers visit either one. There are plans to begin selling items online, as well as to create hampers which customers can make up for a truly bespoke gift.

MOOKAU

Mookau is an eclectic shop selling fun and unusual gifts: "It's all about things that spark joy; when people stop by it puts a smile on their face and brightens their day."

Husband and wife team Nick and Kitty established the shop in August 2007, when both were stuck in careers they didn't want. The pair were looking for a lifestyle change; they were eager to work for themselves and create something new. With this ambition in place, they could see that Sheffield was lacking in stores showcasing cool and independent brands, and from this idea Mookau was formed, nestled in the hustle and bustle of Ecclesall Road.

The store opened to immediate success. By displaying many products made within the city, they managed to strike a chord with the locals, celebrating everything unique that Sheffield has to offer. "I love that since we're small we can reflect what customers want, having the flexibility to adapt and keep selections fresh", Kitty tells us. "As long as it's lovely, we'll sell it!"

Mookau offers a diverse range of items, making sure there's a mix of UK-based, indie companies. They sell over 1000 products, including jewellery from Stella and Wolf, York-based Choc Affair chocolates, and a variety of vegan bath products. All the bath and body products are 90% handmade, and they also have a fantastic vegan range, priding themselves on their inclusivity. Sheffield-based products include The Colours of Sheffield, which is the bestselling range – people love to have that local connection to the city! Based in S7, Beth Pegler is also hugely popular, a handmade textile jewellery range perfect for gifting to loved ones.

2020 was a difficult year for all, and with this in mind they created a lockdown scheme, writing and sending cards for those who could not see their loved ones. During this time, Kitty wrote hundreds of heartfelt messages, realising the importance of frivolity during times of isolation. There is value in Mookau's ethos; gift-giving brings people together, which has become especially relevant in lockdown. It's important for them to give back to the community, and they have given 10% of the sales they make from face coverings to Roundabout, a youth homelessness charity, with the aim of giving a slice back to those suffering most in the face of the pandemic.

"Thank you to those that continue to support us" says Kitty. "Looking ahead we hope to keep on keeping on, continuing to bring new and exciting products to an ever-changing market."

Mookau
391 Ecclesall Road,
Sheffield, S11 8PG
0114 266 8994
@mookau
mookau.co.uk

SHEFFIELD MAKERS WINTER GARDEN

You'll find the Sheffield Makers Winter Garden shop inside the famous arched glasshouse in the heart of the city centre. They exclusively sell items by artists, designers and makers living in the Steel City — who all work together to run the store.

"Sheffield has a thriving creative scene with many studio spaces and independent creative industries — though until recently it felt like that happened out of sight and hidden from the world," says founder Kate Cooper. "The shop is our little way of showing off some of Sheffield's creativity to locals and visitors, coinciding with a general cultural swing towards celebrating makers and creatives."

It all began quite accidentally in 2015. The space was advertised during the middle of November for a December pop-up and Kate took on the challenge with just one week to plan, gathering a band of creatives she had met or bought from at craft markets while selling her own work.

"It was too big a space for just me, so I wanted to pull in as many other Sheffield creatives I could think of," she explains. Between them they begged and borrowed from friends and family for unused dining tables, clothes rails, shelves, and other displays for the shop. Kate describes the mad dash to pull it all together as feeling like an episode of The Apprentice ("except that everyone was lovely!").

They decked the place out in just one day ready for the Christmas season. Following an exhausting but successful month the opportunity came to take on the unit permanently and they decided to jump at it. "It's been a life-changing learning curve working out how to run a collaborative retail business from scratch. It's a juggling act, but we've formed some great relationships and have enough skills and energy between us to make everything work."

Thankfully, their hard work has paid off, and Sheffield Makers is now a popular fixture on the city's independent retail scene. "We've seen the shop develop into a vibrant offering of talent. We sell a whole range of work that's made here and get to show it off to all the folk that visit. We get to experience so much of Sheffield's cultural life as visitors come here for the snooker, Doc/Fest, and Off The Shelf. I never realised how many tourists the city gets!"

Many different makers have joined over the last five years — sometimes permanently, sometimes for a short-term guest spot. New creative pieces are always welcome, and Kate and the team constantly have their eyes peeled for what's out there. "We are always on the look-out for new folk, especially those offering something we haven't got. We're always drawn to colour, interest and sustainability." Visit for Sheffield made jewellery, art, cards, homewares, clothes or shop online at sheffieldmakerswintergardens.com.

Sheffield Makers
Winter Garden
90 Surrey Street
S1 2LH

SHEFFIELD MAKERS HUNTERS BAR

In 2018, some of the team from Sheffield Makers Winter Gardens saw an opportunity for a setting up a larger sister store in the old Jesters on Ecclesall Road. One of their team had stocked jewellery in Jesters when it first opened and brought the idea forward to some of the other stockists.

"The building has had an interesting history," says co-founder Steph. "It was originally a family-run bakery with ovens still hidden in the walls. It was then bought by the current owner, Michael, who ran it as an interior design shop with his late wife, Janice, and their sons. It had always been a dream of Janice's to use part of it as a studio and retail space for artists. It was lovely to learn that we are carrying on a bit of her legacy and vision some 50 years later. It then became the much-loved gift and toy shop Jesters before sitting empty."

It was decided to set up the sister store as a completely separate business from the Winter Garden shop so the two places could evolve in whatever ways worked for them. Such a big leap needed new finances and a larger team, so it made sense to be independent. Sheffield Makers Hunters Bar was the result, and today it stocks products from over 50 different local creative businesses.

When it comes to an effective ethos, Steph is keen to emphasise how teamwork and a commitment to the city's creative community runs through the very core of what they do. "Running your own creative business can be quite an isolating experience, but coming together works so well. None of us could do this on our own, but together we share out the staffing and offer shoppers a vibrant mix of items while still running our own projects. Our commitment to only stocking Sheffield-made things means that folk are buying directly from someone very local. It's a great relationship on both sides."

The store couldn't be better placed than in the Sharrow Vale area of the city – a hive of independent businesses where you can easily spend the day browsing interesting places and eating well. "We have had so much support from folk since setting up our Hunters Bar sister shop. People are so receptive to supporting local. Every day brings new conversations – and we get to meet some great dogs too!" Sheffield Makers Hunters Bar sits on the corner of Hunters Bar roundabout. You can visit (with dogs) or online at sheffieldmakershuntersbar.com.

Sheffield Makers
Hunters Bar
667 Ecclesall Road,
Sharrow,
Sheffield S11 8PT
sheffieldmakershuntersbar.
com

RETAILERS

Get your hands on quality products while supporting local business. Here are some more of our favourite independent retailers dotted around the city.

Jojo's General Store // instagram.com/ragparadesheffield
A fascinating treasure trove decked out with an assortment of gear, ranging from the Victorian era to the 90s, and rated as one of the top vintagewear spots in the country.

Beanies // beanieswholefoods.co.uk
Beanies is a busy wholefoods shop and greengrocers in Walkley who've been going since 1986. They sell fruit and vegetables (organic and non-organic), wholefoods, fresh bread, chilled and frozen produce, snacks and drinks, and continental and speciality foods including gluten-free and dairy-free. Something for everyone, here.

Bailey of Sheffield // baileyofsheffield.com
Bailey of Sheffield creates engineered stainless steel jewellery to last more than a lifetime, allowing its customers to curate their own unique style on a solid steel foundation. It's gone global too, with BOS stocking in stores over the pond in Canada.

A Month of Sundays // petemckee.com
Celebrated Sheffield artist Pete McKee and his timeless works depicting the culture of the city are institutions here. Naturally, his gallery shop, A Month Of Sundays, can be found on the home of independents, Sharrow Vale Road. Also naturally, it isn't open on a Sunday...

Vulgar // vulgarsheffield.com
Taking inspiration from past sub-cultures, Vulgar vintage store specialises in one-of-a-kind jazzy patterns and prints, statement festival pieces, early 90s and 00s designer labels and timeless accessories, plus all the go-to classic wardrobe staples like leather and denim.

Kelham Arcade // kelhamarcade.uk
Once an abandoned industrial unit, the now-thriving Kelham Arcade at 92 Burton Road exemplifies the area's transformation from largely derelict suburb to hotspot for independent business, creative workspaces and retail. Inside you'll find Kelham Barber, Reyt Good Illustration, Purdy's Hair Salon, Crybaby Tattoo, and Gloss Nail Studio.

J H Mann // facebook.com/ JHMannFinestFishmongers

Sheffield's about as far from the coast as you can get, but this specialist fishmonger on Sharrow Vale Road makes sure that spanking fresh fish and seafood is available all year round. There's even a small seating area in the window where visitors can enjoy hot dishes prepared and cooked then and there. J H Mann are also at Sheffield's newest food hall, Kommune, and are soon to have their very own restaurant.

Bear Tree Records // beartreerecords.com

One of many cracking record stores in Sheffield, Bear Tree moved to its unit inside The Forum on Devonshire Street in 2018. Owner Joe Blanchard has worked in record shops for over a decade, with stints at Selectadisc in Nottingham, Jacks Records (formerly Division St) and Record Collector in Broomhill. Safe to say, he knows his stuff and stocks an enviable collection of indie, punk, psych, jazz, techno, soul, folk, metal, and even the odd film soundtrack.

VENUES

everything is different today

SIDNEY&MATILDA

Situated in the up-and-coming Cultural Industries Quarter, Sidney&Matilda combines underground basement bar, art gallery, grassroots music venue and social hangout.

Taking visual cues from Berlin to Brooklyn, this innovative venue is housed in a century-old former paper factory. Opened back in August 2018, visitors have been wowed by events featuring hundreds of regional, national and international artists and creatives.

Undeterred by recent pandemic problems, the venue re-launched in collaboration with soon-to-be demolished Café Totem in the summer, with an eclectic line-up of cultural events including live music, comedy, football & more – providing a ray of hope for the city's social scene during a difficult period and giving us all a glimpse of its potential for the future.

It's been a tough year, but owner Al Daw tells us he is optimistic about the future. "Having worked on the building for almost two years, converting a damp factory with one lightbulb into a fully-fledged grassroots live music venue, we won't let a pandemic stop us. We are in a great location, a five-minute walk from the station and a stone's throw from the Leadmill. There's so much potential and creative talent in this city that we want to host and promote; we are ambitious and really want to push our presence beyond the region, inviting not just artists but also fans from further afield.

Rivelin Works, S1 4RH
@sidneyandmatilda
sidneyandmatilda.com